Leadership Lessons Learned From Muammar Gaddafi

By Lisa Gibson

Leadership Lessons Learned From Muammar Gaddafi

Published by the Peace and Prosperity Alliance
www.conflictcoach.biz

The book is dedicated to all people who are victims of oppression, injustice and terrorism at the hands of leaders around the world. May you continue to push against the grain of evil and stand up and lead in a way that is just.

Table of Contents

Introduction

Throughout the last 25 years I have been on an amazing journey. It was a journey that began on that fateful day, December 21, 1988, when my brother was murdered along with 269 other people in the terrorist bombing of Pan Am Flight 103 over Lockerbie, Scotland. It turned my life upside down as it catapulted me on a path, for the first 25 years of my adult life that I would not have chosen for myself. It has been incredible, while also being difficult and often a lonely path. For me, that chapter of my life is coming to close on the 25th anniversary on December 21, 2013. I have learned a tremendous amount about leadership during this season. A study of leadership would be incomplete without an understanding of what not to do in leadership.

Muammar Gaddafi's life collided with mine on December 21, 1988, when he killed my brother. He became the archenemy in my story. But instead of taking on my enemy in the typical way that happens in so many stories, I took a much different approach. I made a choice that I refused to become like him. Instead, I chose to take a path that was the antithesis of his journey. What better way to end this season than show what I have learned about leadership by chronicling Gaddafi's life? So, this book is about what I have learned in how not to lead from watching his life.

In a world that most often seems to honor powerful people, many of whom abuse, oppress and take advantage of people to achieve their purposes, I wanted to communicate a different message. I wanted to show the dark side of leaders. Throughout history, we chronicle stories of powerful people who have been made famous for their bad deeds. There isn't a person who doesn't know of Hitler, Saddam Hussein, and countless others. Yet, none of them left a positive legacy.

This book is an attempt to share some of my journey and how it drastically differs from the likes of Gaddafi. To some my path has been seen as absurd or naïve. Yet, I know in my heart that it is the right path and the only path that can truly change the world we live in.

On my journey, I have traveled around the world sharing my story and teaching conflict resolution in war-torn nations such as Afghanistan, Libya, Iraq and Sudan. I have become a leader by being a servant. I have been given the opportunity to speak into the lives of leaders of many nations, simply because I chose to follow the path of good rather than evil. I realized that the only way to overcome evil, is with good. When people see that kind of good they are drawn to it. Time and again, people tell me that my story is compelling, inspiring, and even convicting, but in a gentle way. They see that the path I am on, is the truth path of leadership. My role models are the likes of Jesus, Martin Luther King Jr., Nelson Mandela, Mother Teresa. These are all true servant leaders who modeled the truth path of leadership through the simplicity of their lives and service and by the message that they communicated. Love triumphs over evil. They each, in their own way, knew what it was to live, love and make a difference. They made a difference, leaving this earth better off than when they came. They didn't store up riches on earth, but in heaven. They also suffered. They didn't take the easy path, but often took the more difficult path, because they saw that more fruit would be reaped there. They were not cowardly, but courageous. They were true world changers even though many of them did not hold positions of great power or prestige.

I was honored this year to receive the distinction of joining all of these role models above in being chosen as an Exemplar of Love and Forgiveness in Governance by the Fetzer Institute and School for Conflict Resolution at George Mason University. It was a tremendous honor to receive such an accolade and to be chosen to join this select class of people, who take the road less traveled and respond in love and forgiveness. In this life, if you follow the road less traveled, you may not be rewarded with accolades and that cannot be your motivation. You must be motivated by truth and righteousness, because the path isn't easy and there are obstacles along the way that will attempt to hinder you from achieving your objective. Often the only kudos you will receive when you choose the true path of leadership, is an internal sense of peace. This peace will be your guiding compass when the world turns on you or criticizes you for your path. People will condemn you and chastise you because they have chosen to follow the easy path. Their path is the path many leaders in the world have followed and still follow.

The path that is self-centered, not love-centered. Many who have followed the truth path, haven't lived to reap the rewards. Instead, some paid the price with their lives. Many didn't even receive much recognition until they died.

Most of the internal fortitude for pursuing this direction must come from deep within and from a spiritual connection. Some have described my journey as the moral high ground. I can think of no better call to a world that has seen so many low points and so much immoral and unjust behavior among many world leaders. Maybe it is time for a new generation of leaders, those who pursue righteousness, justice, peace and service as the highest call. These ideas and principles are not ones that often receive much press or coverage in television shows or movies. Yet, in the end, they are the ones that truly impact the world.

My hope is that as you read this book, it will be a teaching tool and encouragement on the true path and attributes of leaders that we should all strive for. I also hope that you will see that not only can you make a difference in this world, you have an obligation to. The most direct route to the true path of leadership, is to walk in the opposite direction of those who have abused their leadership and left destruction in their wake. There is much we can learn from history and stories of bad leaders that give light into how easy it is for leaders to get off track and end up causing evil to the people they are called to serve.

Rather than bending into this destructive leadership, I choose to stand against it and I hope you will too. He who passively accepts evil is as much involved in it as he who helps to perpetrate it. As Martin Luther King Jr. once said, "He who accepts evil without protesting against it is really cooperating with it." Let us never again follow the path of evil, but instead lead a course as leaders in the direction of virtue.

Chapter 1: Destinies collide

"I would like to interrupt our regular programming to bring this important announcement," the reporter declared.

Sitting in a comfy chair watching my favorite shows I was a bit annoyed.

Why do these interruptions always come during my favorite shows and right at a really important part?

"We have just received news that a Boeing 747 has gone down over the town of Lockerbie in southern Scotland."

I popped up from my chair as I listened intently to the newscaster explain how a plane on its way from London had blown up over Scotland after leaving from London Heathrow on its way to the United States. The pictures were horrific, debris everywhere, buildings on fire and sirens blaring. It was chilling to watch.

My heart sunk as I paused to think about those poor people and their families who had lost their loved ones just days before Christmas. My heart went out to them as I allowed myself to sit there, glued to the television screen.

For a brief moment, I remembered the picture I had seen the night before as I lay in bed. I was thinking about my brother's impending return home the following day. And as I lay there, a picture flashed before my eyes of a plane exploding in the air.

Ugh, why would I think such a thing?

I forced the picture from my mind and lay there feeling guilty for even "imagining" such a thing.

I got chills.

"Oh my God!" I declared loudly "How weird is it that I would see that picture last night and this happened."

But no one was around to hear me.

Yet, even as I sat there watching the events unfold on television, I never even suspected. Not for one moment, that my brother Ken could have been on that plane. After all, he was coming from Germany, not London.

Instead, in that moment, my focus was on "those people" who had lost their family that fateful night.

Like most people, when tragedies strike, I said a prayer for the victims and their loved ones and remained glued to the television for hours as the events unfolded.

In much the same way that 9/11 impacted the world years later, every television station was covering the tragedy. There must be something innate in us as humans. Like when all the drivers slow down at the scene of an accident to see if they can see anything. It isn't about objectification, but concern on one level and curiosity on the other.

My mom had taken the day off from work and was in the kitchen busy making Ken's favorite dish, Mom's spaghetti.

She walked into the living room where I sat glued to the television.

"There has been a plane crash," I said.

Mom shared how she had gotten two calls from friends telling her about this. The first call was from Olivia, her longtime childhood friend.

"What time is Ken supposed to get in?" Olivia asked.

"Around 4 p.m.," my mother said. "I don't know the specifics, but he plans to call when he arrives at the airport. Why?"

"Oh no reason," she responded.

Since our family lived only five minutes from the airport, my parents didn't even think twice about the fact that Ken hadn't given them a flight itinerary. We only knew he was coming from Berlin and the approximate time he was supposed to arrive.

Within an hour, the phone rang again. This time it was a woman from Mom's work, named Patty Cooper. It was strange for Patty to call Mom during the workday from the office.

"What time is Ken coming in and what flight is he on?" Patty asked.

"Why are you wondering all this?" Mom responded, starting to become concerned.

Patty explained that her husband had called her at work, saying he had seen a news story on television about a plane that had crashed in the British Isles. But Patty tried to reassure Mom that Ken probably wasn't on the plane.

Since these were the days before 24-hour news coverage on television, we waited until the noon hour and I flipped through the stations until I found a news show. The lead story was about a plane that had gone down in Lockerbie. But the details at that point were still pretty hazy. Everyone on board had been killed.

The news reported that it was a Pan American jumbo jet bound from London to New York that had slammed into a gasoline station and a row of houses in a small town of 2,500 residents 15 miles north of the English border, igniting a fireball that rose 300 feet into the sky. The fuselage from the plane left a crater in the ground approximately 20 feet deep and 100 feet long.

Mom tried to do the math in her head to figure out the probability with flight time and distance if there was any chance that Ken could have been on that plane.

He would have had to have been on an earlier flight to be here by 4 p.m., Mom thought.

The news reported that the plane had been on a layover to Heathrow Airport in London. The plane had left Heathrow at 6:25 p.m. local time, and the last contact from the crew was at 7:15 p.m., when the plane was cruising at 31,000 feet. That Flight 103 originated in Frankfurt as a Boeing 727 and changed to a 747 at Heathrow, where additional passengers boarded.

The plane was only half full with 243 passengers and a crew of 15, and it was scheduled to land at New York's John F. Kennedy International Airport at 9:19 p.m. The flight was to end in Detroit.

Numb to what I was seeing, I sat on the couch dazed with confusion. All I could think about was the vision I had the night before. *Oh please, no, God!* I was overcome with guilt. *Please God, no, I will do anything you ask me if you please make this not true.*

The news reported that, as rescue teams reached the crash scene, there were indications of an explosion aboard the plane. The jet's cabin door was found about 10 miles from the rest of the cockpit, while an engine was found on a highway outside town. The one intact piece of the aircraft to fall to the ground was the nose cone, flight deck and forward part of the first-class cabin, which was ripped off from the rest of the fuselage by the force of explosion.

We waited for more details, vacillating between concern for the victims' family members and worry about the possibility that Ken might have been on board.

Our small townhouse was located directly across the street from Detroit Metropolitan Airport. We had grown accustomed to the sound of planes flying low over our home as they were coming in for a landing. But today it was different. *I wonder if that's Ken's flight.* Each plane that flew over drew my attention like it never had before.

The 4 o'clock hour came and went, and we heard nothing from Ken. Mom paced the floors nervously. My brothers Eric and Jason had gotten home from school and we all sat anxiously awaiting any updates that might be forthcoming on the 5 o'clock news. Any hope that we had clung to was quickly eroding away.

Around 5:30 p.m. my father came home from work. Mom told him about the news that we had so far and that Ken had not called her to come pick him up.

This was the first time Dad had heard of the tragedy. In his typical take-charge fashion, he grabbed the phone and dialed Pan Am Airlines. He paced back and forth while waiting, hoping to reach a human being. When Dad finally got through to a customer service representative, she simply confirmed that Ken was listed on the flight manifest.

We all huddled around the phone, waiting for the answer.

"Oh my God, he was on the plane," he exclaimed before breaking down in tears. My mom and two younger brothers started weeping as well.

But I remained unemotional, unwilling to believe Ken had been on the plane. "Maybe they're wrong," I said.

Dad immediately called the airline back to get more details. Somewhere within that five-minute timeframe, airline officials pulled the manifest and prohibited the agents from confirming who was and wasn't on board the flight. The next customer service representative refused to release any details, including whether Ken was even on the flight manifest.

Dad became furious. "They just told me my son was on that plane," he yelled into the phone.

"Official notification has to come from an official Pan Am Airlines representative," the agent said.

This threw us into confusion. Was Ken on the plane or not? I calmly held out hope, while the rest of my family gave into a myriad of emotions, from anger to grief. That moment I felt like I was having an out-of-body experience, like watching a movie, not living a real-life nightmare.

Maybe he just missed his flight. Maybe he is safe but can't get to a phone to call us. I'm sure he's fine. I conjured up an image in my mind of Ken wandering the streets of Germany, looking for a way to get in touch with us.

When faced with trauma, the mind has the incredible ability to create alternate scenarios as a coping mechanism.

As the evening unfolded, Dad must have called the airport nine or ten times trying to get information. Around midnight, we received the official news from the Pan Am 103 representative. Ken had been on the flight.

Mom was surprisingly calm, trying to figure out how to respond. But Dad needed more answers. "Can you confirm whether my son Ken was wearing his military uniform?" he asked the airline representative, thinking that would confirm whether Ken was, indeed, on the plane.

"Your son was in the military?" she said. "Oh my, I wasn't supposed to notify you. I am so sorry. The military is required to notify military family members in person."

Despite having our worst fears confirmed, we were glad the representative called because we didn't receive the official news from the military until mid-afternoon the following day.

That night I didn't sleep much. I was thoroughly exhausted from all that had transpired that day, but I was restless. My mind played back all the images that I had seen that day. It was like a film reel that was on a continual loop, showing the same pictures again, and again—the images of the plane wreckage, the sirens blaring and ambulances flying down streets of the small Scottish town, the fire burning the buildings of Lockerbie and the horrified looks on the faces of the first responders and law enforcement as they released the details of the tragedy.

I imagined what that day must have been like for Ken. Four days before Christmas, my 20-year-old brother, an army specialist, packed the last of his belongings into a medium-size suitcase, before catching a taxi to the airport in Berlin, Germany. It was an exciting day for him, after having been away serving his country for nearly two years. He was heading home to spend Christmas with his family in Michigan. It was to be a long series of flights. First to Frankfurt, then to London Heathrow, and then on to New York City, before finally arriving in Detroit, Michigan.

On December 21, 1988, his flight landed at London Heathrow Airport for refueling. The earlier flight had been

13

overbooked and he was bumped to the later flight. The plane was only half full, so he was looking forward to having some extra room to sleep on the overnight flight to the United States. He boarded the plane with the other passengers and settled into his seat, beaming with anticipation. As he looked out the window at the ground crew going about their business, unbeknownst to anyone a suitcase was being loaded onto the plane, which was different from all the others

The head purser made the announcement over the intercom with the final departure instructions.

"Ladies and gentlemen, I would like to thank you for flying with us today on this 7-hour flight to New York. The last of the luggage is being loaded onto the plane. In a few moments we will be ready to pull away from the gate. Please take your seats and be sure your seat belts are securely fastened and your seats are in the upright position. This is Pan Am Flight 103."

The plane pulled back from the gate, taxied down the runway and revved its engines as it began to lift off from the ground and into the horizon. The young man looked at the ground one last time as it was slowly becoming more and more distant and thought to himself, *this will be the last takeoff before I once again plant my feet firmly on the ground in the United States.*

At 19:00 hours local time, the last communications were heard from the plane. It was at that time that my brother's life became a memory.

I wanted to pinch myself to see if it was real. It was a horrific dream that I desperately wanted to wake up from, but try as I might, I just couldn't shake the depths of it. As I remembered the vision from the night before, my heart sank with guilt. *Did I cause this? Where is God in all of this?*

I felt very alone.

The collision of my life with Gaddafi's

On December 21, 1988, my life collided with that of Muammar Gaddafi, although I didn't know it at the time. It took years for Gaddafi to be identified as the mastermind behind the Lockerbie bombing. Instead, for many years the person responsible for the Lockerbie bombing was a faceless terrorist. Very soon after the bombing, it became clear that it was an act of terrorism with a

bomb bringing down the Boeing 747 over a small town called
Lockerbie in the south of Scotland. That flight was Pan Am Flight
103 bound from London to New York City. Had it not been for the
delay of the flight out of London Heathrow, we might never have
found the remains or evidence that was discovered. But as
providence would have it, the plane was delayed and the bomb,
rigged with a timer, went off shortly before the plane was to reach
the ocean. The culprit had planned the bombing well. Sophisticated
timers were obtained from a Swiss maker and rigged into a Toshiba
BomBeat Radio, then placed in a piece of luggage that traveled
unaccompanied from London. The luggage was found to have
originated in Malta and been checked in by Abdel Basset Al
Megrahi, a Libyan intelligence agent who traveled under and carried
different aliases. Megrahi traveled with the luggage from Malta to
London, but did not board the plane with the luggage in London.

Early in the case there were alternative theories on who was
responsible for the Lockerbie bombing. Some thought it was Iran,
others the Palestinians. One of the initial suspects was Ahmed Jibril,
a known Palestinian terrorist who was close to Gaddafi and had
received support from Gaddafi for his work.

Several years into the investigation, the evidence led the
Scottish government and other agencies assisting with the
investigation to Libya, and Megrahi and Al Amin Khalifah Fhimah,
who was the director of Libya's airlines office in Malta, were
charged. But it took years of pressure on Gaddafi for him to turn
them over for trial.

I was 18 years old and a freshman in college when my
brother became one of the casualties of the Lockerbie terrorist
attack. Within minutes my simple sheltered existence was shaken to
the core as my family was thrust into the public eye in such a high-
profile way. Everyone around the world was talking about the
Lockerbie bombing and wanted our perspective. As an 18-year-old I
wasn't prepared to deal with the magnitude of this type of tragedy.
Are you ever really prepared for tragedy? But when it is something
like this, such a senseless act of violence directed against innocent
people, it brings you to your knees. You no longer have the capacity
to see the world as safe or people as good. For me, I was thankful to
have an internal moral fortitude that was firmly grounded in my

Christian faith. It was a senseless act of violence where my brother was taken from our family. We did not get to say goodbye, or share the things we had been hoping to share with him since he had been away serving the U.S. in Germany for two years. He was coming home for Christmas, a time that to most is associated with hope, joy, peace, redemption. But instead, that time came to represent death, loss, grief and evil for my family and the other victims' family members.

When the Lockerbie bombing happened on December 21, 1988, we had already made plans to spend the Christmas holiday with my grandparents up in Northern Michigan. We were all looking forward to seeing Ken and the joy of spending Christmas with him. Days after the bombing we had no answers or any clear sense of when we would even get answers let alone get Ken's body back for the funeral. So, we packed our bags and went to Grandma's house hoping to somehow salvage some semblance of Christmas. But despite being together as a family, it was an incredibly sad and grim time. I couldn't muster even the appearance of joy that Christmas. As I look back at the pictures of our family in front of the Christmas tree, I wonder why we even took those pictures. We all looked so sad because our hearts were broken into a thousand pieces. Even looking at the picture today can cause those feelings of deep sorrow to come rushing to the surface again. It was grim.

On December 21, 1988, Gaddafi stole our Christmas. He stole our peace and joy. But what he could not steal was the redemption in that tragedy. For many years to come, Christmas was associated with Lockerbie, my brother's death and sorrow. While many around the world began moving into the holiday cheer, I saw Christmas as a somber time and ever-present reminder of my loss. For years we still had no answers or knowledge of who was responsible, just more questions as the years passed. As a result of that, there was no closure, there was no peace. Every year as the anniversary of Lockerbie came, it was just a depressing reminder of our loss and the lack of resolution. For years the victims' families watched as Gaddafi refused to turn over Fhimah and Megrahi for trial. It was like a slap in our faces. *At least give us the chance to find out the truth, I thought to myself.* But of course, as we later found, that truth would implicate Gaddafi for this crime, so like any good coward Gaddafi was protecting himself. I imagined him sitting in his palace or his tent in a desert someplace laughing about what he had done. There was no remorse, no sorrow for what he had done. Instead, I imagined him rejoicing about how he hurt America. The victims were nameless faces in his mind, collateral damage in Gaddafi's plan of revenge. Gaddafi's goal was to take down capitalism and Western influences around the world. The motive was believed to be retaliation for the U.S. air raid on Libya in 1986. The U.S. sent an air strike to target Gaddafi's governmental buildings after Gaddafi bombed a Berlin disco, killing several U.S. soldiers. In a blatant disregard for human life Gaddafi attacked innocent civilians while the U.S. struck back by attacking governmental institutions. In retaliation, Gaddafi attacked innocent civilians again. There were no "rules of war" for Gaddafi. Instead he intentionally attacked noncombatants. Only a coward plays the game this way.

That was Gaddafi's character as was confirmed by nearly everyone who knew him. He was a sociopath who hated everyone and loved only himself. Gaddafi had no remorse about killing and torturing Libyan citizens, so why would he feel remorse about harming other people? It was clear, as the world looked on, that he had no conscience. He raped, stole and murdered at will without even showing a tiny sense of remorse

As an 18-year-old when this tragedy happened, I was truly in my most formative years. I was trying to figure out who I was and the path that my life would take. For over a year I struggled through a deep depression, trying to make any sense of my brother's death. Of course there was none. It was senseless and malicious. Despite my despair, I refused to allow bitterness to overcome me. Instead, I took my anger and grief to God. I wrestled with him through all my questions. For a time, my faith was deeply shaken. How could a good God allow such a thing to happen? Why me? Why didn't God stop it? As I was wrestling through these questions for almost a year, we didn't even know who to blame so I channeled all my anger at God. And He carried me through that.

As I started to pull myself out of the deep place of sorrow I had lived in for that year, I began to think proactively. I realized I could not bring my brother back, but I also realized that maybe there was a way to prevent terrorism and a tragedy like this again. I even ended up doing my senior thesis on Islamic terrorism, hoping that would give me some answers on why someone would do something like this. I studied the ins and outs of terrorism throughout history, paralleling terrorism in places like Ireland and the Middle East. What I found is that at the heart of terrorism is hate and fear. Terrorists attack innocent people to create fear and chaos and communicate an ideological message. Terrorism was not rooted in anything sane or just. It was completely counter to the principles of just war. At its very core is wickedness. So, I realized, as I looked at terrorists around the world committing these horrific acts, that they think they have power, but have none. I realized that if at the heart of terrorism is hate and fear, the only way to effectively fight it is to walk in the opposite spirit of love and faith. I realized that I could not fight the battle with the enemy's weapons. The only way to truly lead this fight against terrorism and the likes of Gaddafi was to take a completely different path.

Gaddafi's life became the antithesis of the life that I would lead from that day forth. His leadership style represented everything young people should aspire not to be. In a world that honors power at any cost, self-centeredness, abuse, I chose to walk a different path. I chose to follow the path of light and not of darkness. Following the path of revenge only leads to death and destruction, starting with destruction from the inside out. My journey began with a decision to forgive all the terrorists responsible for my brother's death, which included Megrahi and Fhimah. At first it was an intellectual decision, but as I walked it out the feelings began to come.

The aftermath

I wish I could say that we recovered from this tragedy quickly. But the answer would be far from the truth.

I walked around in a haze for several weeks upon returning to college after Christmas break. The Lockerbie tragedy was the talk of the town and our campus. While every professor was talking about it and integrating it into our lectures in class, I was trying desperately to forget the nightmare.

It was only when my brother's body was returned home for his funeral and I saw him lying there in the casket that my world began to unravel.

Muammar Gaddafi stole my brother that day and the lives of 269 other people. He also nearly destroyed my family. I sunk into a deep depression and struggled deeply for nearly a year to pull myself out of it. He also destroyed my parents' marriage. Initially, my brother's death brought our family closer, but when the dust settled it ended up causing our family to implode.

I directed my anger toward God. *Why did he allow this to happen? How could a good God let bad things happen to good people?* It was in that time of the deepest and darkest moments of my soul, that God carried me and listened to laments. He picked me up from that place of brokenness and showed me how to make beauty from ashes.

Despite walking through the valley of the shadow of death for almost a year, I came out of that dark time stronger and more resilient. Every tragedy that we as humans experience breaks us. They bring us to our knees and we have a choice, we can let go of the pain or hold onto it until a root of bitterness is born. That root is where revenge spurs from. For some the revenge is something that happens merely in their thoughts. But for others, the revenge flows out of our heart in anger and violence toward others. For some the violence is perpetrated against the person that hurt us, but for others, it ends up being directed at others in our lives. Sometimes we even hurt people we love very deeply.

Unresolved anger is deeply destructive. The roots of many of societies' problems can be traced to a spirit of revenge or people enslaved to a retaliatory cycle. The only way to break the cycle, is for one person to choose to walk in the opposite spirit. Rather than allowing anger and bitterness to consume us, we choose to forgive.

For me, this process can best be described through a legal analogy. When we have an offense or hurt, that issue tends to consume our thoughts. Maybe for a moment we can briefly forget about it, but invariably, when we are left to our own thoughts again, those emotions come rushing to the surface again. It is as if we are litigating the wrong done to us in the inner courtroom of our heart and can find no relief. There is no peace. The only way to find the personal peace we desire, is to take the wrong done to us and transfer it to heaven's courtroom and let God deal with it.

At the age of 18, I gained a perspective and insight that many have said was well beyond my years. I believe it was divine wisdom that there was a way to take my pain and channel it into something life-giving and meaningful. For me, that was to take my brother's death and overcome that act of evil with good. Those simple words, which are rooted in Scripture, have become my mantra for the last 25 years.

I think Scott Peck said it best in his book *The Road Less Traveled*.

"The whole course of human history may depend on a change of heart in one solitary and even humble individual - for it is in the solitary mind and soul of the individual that the battle between good and evil is waged and ultimately won or lost."

So, I made the choice to take the road less traveled; rather than succumbing to bitterness or simple indifference, I chose to respond in love.

I made a decision to take on my nemesis Muammar Gaddafi. While he was engaging in his evil wickedness around the world, I would take a different path. While revenge permeated every ounce of his being, I would allow love to consume me.

It was a simple act of obedience in the beginning, but as I walked it out the feelings came. It was by God's grace, His strength and wisdom that I was able to walk the path I have walked and have the influence I have had. Some have called me courageous. But in truth, the only courage was my willingness to follow the path put before me in faith, trusting that He who is greater than me would show me the way.

If you would have told me 25 years ago, that I would have had the opportunity to do the things I have done throughout the last 25 years, I never would have believed you. Likely, had I known what I know now, I would have shrunk back in fear. But thankfully, I was not given the master plan or how this would all play out. While Gaddafi was scheming and planning his evil escapades, I was simply following the path of peace. I clung close to God and allowed Him to guide my steps.

In the beginning of this journey the culprit for Lockerbie was still a nameless and faceless villain. But as the years passed, and the investigation unfolded, Gaddafi was singled out as the mastermind. There was ultimately a conviction of Abdel Basset Al Megrahi, a Libyan intelligence agent, an acceptance of responsibility by Libya and a payment of civil damages. But the story doesn't end there.

For me, the conviction of Abdel Basset Al Megrahi was just the beginning of the real impact I would have. It began with a letter of forgiveness I wrote to Megrahi letting him know that I had chosen to forgive him. He replied to my letter in early July 2004.

Shortly after receiving Megrahi's reply, I reached out to the Libyan Ambassador to the U.S. Ali Aujali, after he opened the Libya Interest Office in Washington, D.C. In late 2004, he helped facilitate a personal reconciliation trip for me to Libya. I shared with him that I needed to go to Libya because I wanted to see the Libyans differently than I was seeing them. I didn't want to see them all as terrorists. I was the first Lockerbie family member to go to Libya.

My plan was to meet with as many people as possible. I even requested a meeting with Muammar Gaddafi. He chose not to, but I did meet with his senior cabinet officials. I wasn't disappointed that I didn't meet Gaddafi on that visit, because I had a clear vision that I would one day meet him.

It was a profound experience for me to meet the people, share my story and build a bridge of reconciliation. What I found was a people that for years had been told Lockerbie never happened, yet there they were confronted with a woman who said not only did it happen, but my brother was killed. If that were not enough, I came to Libya because I wanted to meet them so I could find a way to forgive and love them. As you can imagine, the responses were ones of shock. Several of my new Libyan friends shared that they thought Americans hated them.

My response was, "How could we hate you, we don't even know you."

I found out that there was power in loving your enemies that breaks down all kinds of wrong patterns of thought and stereotypes we have about people of different cultures and religions.

The confirmation of the importance of my trip came from the feedback I received from my new friends.

One of my guides said, "I will do everything I can to help you."

As I shared my story, it created an opportunity for the people to explain secretly what their lives were like. I learned first-hand some of the horror stories and oppression that they lived with for the first time. It wasn't until the Libyan revolution several years later that the rest of the world heard their stories.

21

I left Libya committed to help. I realized, I could not bring my brother back, but could help people who were still suffering at the hands of Gaddafi. That was the most tangible example of how I could overcome evil with good. Within a month of my filing the incorporation documents with the IRS, our nonprofit was approved. That was unheard of and what I believed to be a miracle and a sign.

Without a clue of how to begin, I approached Ambassador Aujali and let him know that I wanted to find a way to build a bridge of reconciliation in Libya. He warmly received that. We started our work in Libya under a Congressional initiative called Adopt-A-Country Caucus. The mission of the Peace and Prosperity Alliance was to deal with the root issues of terrorism, oppression and conflict, by helping developing countries develop.

We ended up working directly with the Gaddafi Development Foundation, which was run by Gaddafi's son Saif Al Islam Gaddafi. We did training projects for English teachers, helped kids in Libya with HIV/Aids, etc. You can read my extraordinary story in entirety in my award-winning best-seller *Life In Death: A Journey From Terrorism To Triumph*, which is being adapted into a screenplay for a movie.

Chapter: 2 Face-to-face

As I settled into my seat on the flight to New York, I was deep in thought. Just days before, Ambassador Aujali had assured me he would do everything in his power to make the meeting between Muammar Gaddafi and myself happen. Having known and worked with Ambassador Aujali for five years, I knew he was cautious by nature. So, when he said he would do everything he could to make it happen, I knew he would. The details were still unclear. I had just booked a flight to New York City in faith, believing that this long-held vision of meeting with Gaddafi would happen.

Could it be this is really going to happen? Ah God, I don't want to do this.

I felt a trepidation in my heart. I hadn't really stopped to process through this. So there I was on a plane bound for New York City feeling my first pang of doubt and fear. Inside I felt like a five-year-old again.

"God, I don't want to do this. I am scared," I said under my breath.

I heard God speak into my heart, "Lisa, you're not having much fun."

I imagined myself as a little girl digging my heels into the ground when I was being asked to do something I really didn't want to do.

Fun, how can this be fun?

"It is just you hanging out with your dad," He said.

"Okay, I will do it. But don't let go of my hand," I conceded.

"What am I going to say to him?" I whispered.

"Just do what Romans 12 says," He answered.

Romans 12 is the scripture that I knew well. It had become my personal roadmap throughout my journey. It had always been the basis for my mission and even talking points in speeches or media interviews. When people would ask me why I was doing what I was doing, I would simply answer "because the Word tells me to." Even as I say these words, it seems overly simplistic. Yet, as a humans, we often complicate things, making excuses why we can't do such and

23

such. While all along God is saying clearly, "be doers of the word, not just hearers."

So, I arrived in New York without a clue of how this whole thing was going to come together. The only thing I had to go on was Ambassador Aujali's commitment to do everything he could to make it happen. When I arrived in New York I sent a text message to Ambassador Aujali asking if he might be able to get me into the United Nations to hear Gaddafi's speech.

The following morning, I had not heard back, so I decided to walk from my hotel to the United Nations building. The streets were packed with limousines from every nation in the world with dignitaries making their way to the United Nations General Assembly. I followed my pocket map as I meandered my way through the streets of New York City. After a while there was a huge traffic backup as I approached the United Nations building. I was never happier to be on foot rather than being stuck in a bumper-to-bumper traffic jam.

As I approached the United Nations building I saw crowds of protesters outside the UN. There were groups from several different countries demonstrating on a variety of issues. Some were from Palestine, Iran and Libya. But as I got closer, I noticed there was a very large stage set up on the lawn and some type of rally going on. So, I decided to check it out. As I approached the side of the stage outside the barricades, there was a member of the Native American community talking.

I wonder what this is.

I looked over and on the stage was the Libyan flag and pictures of Muammar Gaddafi.

Oh, my. This must be a rally that Gaddafi organized in his own honor.

Inside the barricades there appeared to be groups of Libyans joined by African-American men in bow ties, and members of the Native American community in their traditional dress. There must have been at least 1,000 people.

This is an odd group. Gaddafi must have paid these people to be here.

Sure enough, one by one speakers appeared on stage espousing the virtues of Muammar Gaddafi and the wonderful things he had done to support their group. The most notable was a leader of the Nation of Islam, a group of African-American Muslims led by Louis Farrakhan. He gave his apologies for Farrakhan not being able to attend in person.

I overheard some members of Farrakhan's group talking about how they had taken buses to the rally from all over the Midwest and the eastern part of the U.S.

Come to find out, that had also been the case for the Libyans. Most of them were Libyan students who were attending college in America and were asked to come out and support Gaddafi.

There I stood in the middle of that crowd, the lone white woman amidst a crowd of diverse groups, all of whom had received significant financial support from Muammar Gaddafi.

As I stood there, I pulled out my cell phone to take some pictures for posterity's sake.

Maybe I should send a message to Ambassador Aujali to let him know I am here, in hopes I would be able to get into the UN.

So, I sent a quick text to the Ambassador letting him know I was at Gaddafi's rally. To my surprise he immediately texted me back.

"Hi Lisa. After Gaddafi's speech, we will contact you."

Okay, I still have no idea where or when, but at least we have progress.

Shortly before Gaddafi's speech a man from the Nation of Islam started handing out green-and-white umbrellas and T-shirts that commemorated Gaddafi's first trip to the U.S.

After Gaddafi's speech a group of Libyan youth led a procession or parade of the participants to the Libyan UN mission. The rumor was Gaddafi was planning to meet people there.

So, I followed the crowd, taking in the sights and sounds of what I was witnessing. I just tagged along with the crowd, not wanting to give the impression that I was supporting Gaddafi. Another group of Libyans came up from behind protesting against Gaddafi. I met one young man who told me he was a great-grandson of the Libyan King Idris who was ousted by Gaddafi's coup.

After waiting for what seemed like hours for Gaddafi and no word from the Ambassador, I decided it was time to go get some lunch. So, I called my friend who lived in New York City.

We met up at a local coffee shop as I caught her up on the day's events. She was a great encouragement for me and my efforts.

Ring, ring, my phone chirped.

"Oh, my gosh, it is him," I declared.

"Take it," she said.

"Hello, Lisa. How are you?" Ambassador Aujali asked.

"I am fine, Ambassador, thank you," I said.

"We would like you to come to the Libyan UN Mission tonight at 7 p.m.," he said.

"Great. I will see you then," I said with excitement.

My friend and I finished up our lunch and she sent me off with a brief prayer for encouragement. I headed back to my hotel to get ready for this fateful meeting. I almost had to pinch myself to believe it was really going to happen. I had no fear, but a sense of expectation that something good was going to happen.

I left with plenty of time to get to the Libyan mission by 7 p.m., or at least I thought. I walked from my hotel to the main intersection and stood at the corner trying to hail a taxi. There were lots of taxis passing by, but they were all full. The streets were more packed than usual with the influx of UN participants. I must have waited for at least twenty minutes to no avail.

It is too late to try to figure out where the subway is and to navigate getting to the Libyan Mission. I am just going to start walking and hopefully find a taxi on my way.

So, I took off down the street toward the Libyan Mission. I decided to just walk with my hand up in the air, the common sign for hailing a cab in New York City. Maybe by some small chance a taxi driver would see it.

I had been walking for ten minutes when a black unmarked limosine pulled up and the driver rolled down his window.

"Where are you going?" he asked.

"The Libyan UN mission," I said as I showed him the address on the map.

"I will take you there for $20," he said.

"Perfect," I said not even hesitating for a moment.

Since I felt I was on a divine mission, I had no intention of letting something like transportation hinder my purposes. I sensed God agreed and that was why He sent the car for me.

The limo took off across town, with my urging him to hurry, as I didn't want to be late. When we got within two blocks of the mission, we hit a major traffic jam.

26

Like a scene out of a movie I said, "I am going to go ahead and jump out here and walk the rest of the way. I can't be late."

I handed the driver the twenty, jumped out of the taxi and started walking very quickly down the street. I looked at my watch and the time read 6:50 p.m. I picked up my pace to almost a slow jog. It was September in New York City and humid. The last thing I wanted to do was end up at the meeting sweating profusely. More than that, I didn't want to be late. The only thing I could hope was that he was running late.

When I reached the building, I was out of breath. There was a security detail in place. As I approached the entrance, I had to confirm my name and show some identification. Turned out that the guy standing in front of me, Raymond Pagnucco, was also there to meet Gaddafi. I had not met him before, but we quickly became acquainted in the waiting room. His father had been killed on Pan Am 103 and he had only just begun his journey of reconciliation.

There I stood face-to-face with Muammar Gaddafi, one of the world's most notorious terrorists and the man responsible for my brother's death. As I walked into the meeting room there were Libyans from the UN and security bustling about. This makeshift room was thrown together when Gaddafi was refused in his request to pitch his tent in several different locations around town, and he was denied accommodations at all the hotels in town. Gaddafi was the controversial leader at the UN that year and the talk of the town, especially after his antics earlier in the day at the General Assembly, where his ten-minute speech became an hour-long rambling speech.

Ambassador Aujali led us into the room, and I was the first to meet Gaddafi. He stood up, approached us and shook my hand. I was struck by the sense of complete peace and joy I felt as I shook the hand of the man who murdered my brother. There was no anger, no contempt, no bitterness. It surprised even me as I was experiencing it.

We exchanged pleasantries as the interpreter translated what was being said between us. And then I welcomed Gaddafi to America. Even as I said it, I could hardly believe it myself.

Gaddafi shared his condolences for the loss of our family members, but never went so far as to say he did it.

Raymond and I offered our condolences for the loss of his daughter in the 1986 raid.

27

Then I had the first opportunity to speak. I told him that I had forgiven and was now committed to building bridges of reconciliation with Libya. I shared about the projects I had been doing in Libya with my nonprofit Peace and Prosperity Alliance including projects to help children with HIV/AIDS, English teacher training and the plans we had to do a joint art festival with the U.S. and Libya in collaboration with the foundation of his son Saif Al Islam Gaddafi. He thanked me for the work I was doing.

It was a brief meeting, only about fifteen minutes total. Since I didn't know how much time I would have, I also gave him a card sharing the things I felt led to tell him. It was a Thomas Kinkade card, with one of those idyllic scenes of a log cabin in a majestic mountain setting. To me it exemplified peace. What I shared, both in person and in the card, was what Romans 12 calls us to do. I shared with him that I had forgiven, blessed him, told him about my efforts to serve the Libyan people, and even shared about how I had been praying for him daily. In the card I told him that I had bought a "Gaddafi watch" on my first trip to Libya and said, "Every day I look down at the watch, and I say a prayer for you."

Gaddafi's countenance was very stoic throughout the entire meeting until the end, when I gave him a gift. It was a simple gesture of attempting to do something good to him as the Scripture says. Since I wanted it to have spiritual meaning but also be something he might actually use, I settled on a *Cross* pen. When I gave him the pen, I could tell he was touched. It was the only time he smiled, and he said, "Thank you." As his countenance softened, it was as if for a brief moment I saw his humanity and his heart. God reminded me of the Scripture he gave me for Gaddafi from Proverbs 14:12 that says, "There is a way that seems right to man but its end is the way to death." I thought about who God had desired Gaddafi to be and how very far he had strayed from that path. That meeting was a culmination of many years of striving to see the country of Libya change. It was a long, hard journey that came to a close for me as I sat face-to-face with the man responsible for my brother's death. I told him my desire was to focus on reconciliation with Libya by building a bridge of friendship between the people of the United States and Libya through goodwill and service.

That night as I returned to my hotel, I found myself deep in thought. *What did I actually accomplish there?* I did not know for sure. But I sensed God was very pleased. I felt almost giddy inside. I thought to myself "no one will ever know this happened." There were no media crews, just one single television camera for Libyan television. I figured if people did hear about it, it would be portrayed by Libyan television as something completely different than what actually happened. Little did I know the following evening, as I was flying back to Colorado, Muammar Gaddafi was sharing the story of the meeting on CNN in an interview with Fareed Zakaria. In that interview one of the most notorious terrorists and evil dictator shared how he had been touched by our meeting.

The very next morning, I awoke to my phone ringing off the hook with calls from every major media outlet trying to ascertain if I was the woman who met with Gaddafi. They had gotten my name and contact information from the Libyan Ambassador. The other Lockerbie family members whom they had called denied the story as a fabrication by Gaddafi. "No Lockerbie family member would meet with Gaddafi," some said.

They were wrong. One woman, on a mission of peace, simply trying to love her enemies and overcome evil with good, had chosen to meet with Gaddafi. It was insanity to some and courageous to others. Perhaps it was just the insanity of grace. At a minimum, the path that I have taken is a revolutionary approach when compared with some of the other victims' family members, many who had chosen to focus on bitterness and revenge. Some of those same victims' family members lashed out at me in attacks, claiming that I was misguided or wrong in my approach. Nevertheless, the story of my meeting went around the world and was covered by nearly every large media outlet. CNN was the first to break the story and share my provocative statement that "Love is the most effective weapon in the war on terror." Although there was criticism by some, the positive response far outweighed the negative. My e-mail inbox was flooded with responses from people all over the world who thanked me and asked if there were ways they could help with my work. Many were Muslims and even several Libyans. I believe the response was so positive because when people see unconditional love in action, it is so compelling they are drawn to it. They too see that the only way to confound hate, is to walk in the opposite spirit. On that day, the message that was communicated to the world was simply this: Daily there is a battle being waged between the forces of good and evil through love and hate, but in the end love always wins.

Reconciliation

The completion of the redemptive cycle of overcoming evil with good happened on June 27, 2011, as I spoke to a crowd of 100,000 people in Freedom Square in Benghazi, Libya, on the day the International Court issued the arrest warrant for Muammar Gaddafi. I had gone to Libya to deliver much-needed medical supplies during the heart of the revolution, with my nonprofit called the Peace and Prosperity Alliance. After sharing my story with leaders of the revolution at the courthouse in Benghazi, they asked me to speak at the rally.

As providence would have it, the day that I spoke was the day that the International Court had issued the arrest warrant for Muammar Gaddafi. All day long, there was celebration in the streets. People were waving American flags and signs that said "Thank you Sarkozy" to the French Prime Minister. As we drove down the streets I was caught up in the excitement of it all.

Later that evening, we headed over to the square. The crowd was ten times what it had been like the day before. We could hardly find a parking spot. Even our driver was a bit unnerved about getting our group to the stage safely. So, he called some armed militia members who escorted us through the massive crowd toward the stage. I had never in my life been in a crowd that large. The people were as far as the eye could see.

When we approached the stage there were people leading the crowd in chants and cheers. It was like a giant pep rally. Daily these events were held, to keep the morale of the people up. There were rides for the kids near the waterfront, booths of vendors displaying cultural artifacts, and tents memorializing the martyrs who either died or disappeared during Gaddafi's reign. If I hadn't known any better, I would have thought I was at a fair rather than a rally in the middle of a war. The spirits of the people were very high and celebratory. I could feel the energy of the crowd as I walked through the people. I fed off their excitement and became exhilarated as I approached the stage.

As our group was invited on the stage and they introduced us, the crowd erupted in a huge applause. There were cameras snapping pictures of us. Some in the crowd looked on at us with exhilaration, others with a sense of apprehension. I felt no fear, but was thankful for others in our group who were not quite sure about what we were doing that there were armed militia members standing in front of the stage for our protection. They looked like kids with guns, really. But it was obvious they took their job very seriously.

Everything was being said in Arabic, so I really had no idea of what was being said other than what was communicated through nonverbal communication and emotion. The sentiment that seemed to be expressed was that was a good day to be a Libyan. That their hard work was paying off, and soon they would have the victory that they desired. I sensed a deep heartfelt pride in the people as they united around their common cause. In past visits I had sensed more shame than pride in the people. It was clear they had found their voice, and they had no intention of being quiet ever again. I felt privileged to celebrate that day with them. I felt as though I was experiencing one of those pivotal moments in history, like the fall of the Berlin wall or the freeing of the Jews from concentration camps.

I had not prepared a written speech, trusting that the words would come at the appointed time. Another one of our group shared a brief word of encouragement in Arabic to the people and they erupted in cheers, thankful to see that white American bringing a word of encouragement and greeting in their language.

Our translator approached the podium and began to introduce me. When he said the word "Lockerbie," the crowd immediately grew silent. He had the people's attention.

As I approached the podium, the crowd quieted even more and listened intently. "Salam Alekum," I greeted them in Arabic.

Then I began to share a bit of my story, about losing my brother in the Lockerbie terrorist attack, how I went to Libya in 2004 because I needed to forgive and focus on reconciliation. I shared how that trip was the first time I had heard what their lives were like under Gaddafi, the oppression and abuse. That I had started a nonprofit called the Peace and Prosperity Alliance and had been serving in Libya since 2005 to find a way to improve their lives. Then I simply shared that I came there as a fellow victim of Gaddafi's terror to stand with them during their time of need. To let

31

them know that they were not alone and that there were people all over the world praying for them.

For the first time in all my trips to Libya, I saw the pictures on the wall of martyrs of all the Libyan people who had disappeared or been killed by Muammar Gaddafi, and my heart broke for them. I honestly can't remember all of what I shared but I know I poured out my heart to the people, sharing about my years of serving in Libya and desire to continue helping them, and they were clearly touched. At one point, they interrupted my speech and began chanting, "Thank you, Lisa!" in English. I was so humbled. I was overwhelmed with gratitude and realized how privileged I was to be a part of it. For the first time in my journey, I really understood what I would have missed if I hadn't chosen to follow God down the path of peace.

As I walked through the massive crowd of people with our armored military escorts, I was met with smiles and people wanting to shake my hand and just say "thank you." I felt like a rock star while all along thinking about how grateful I was for God allowing me to be a part of this. The incredibly emotional day ended with a former army general and his sons coming to the hotel where we were staying just to meet me personally and present me with a special award certificate that was fresh off the press. It was one of the most honoring experiences I have ever had. I felt the most blessed I have in my lifetime. Although I went back to Libya to facilitate a leadership institute in January 2012 and again in December 2012, I knew in that moment that the circle of reconciliation came to a close on June 27, 2011.

Story continues

Despite the ending of one chapter, the remainder of my book still remains to be written. Out of the tragedy, I have gained a platform to speak around the world. I have shared my story of reconciliation with Ambassadors from the Middle East at a luncheon in Washington, D.C., and shared the same story with persecuted Christians in the refugee camps of Khartoum, Sudan. The same story, God's story, has been shared time and again around the world. I have also developed a mediation practice and taught conflict resolution to leaders in Afghanistan, Iraq, Libya, Egypt and countless others.

As a result of my loss, I have had the privilege to do peacemaking around the world. In January of 2012, I was facilitating a leadership institute in Benghazi, Libya, the seedbed of the revolution. We were teaching courses in leadership, ethics, project management and conflict resolution. Our hope was to assist with rebuilding Libya by teaching classes that relate to a being a civil society. I had the privilege to teach conflict resolution. As always, as part of the course, I shared my own story and we discussed ways to help Libya to move toward reconciliation and peace. At the break, one of the doctors in the course came up to speak with me. She was a very bright woman who was prone to brashness, and I had already seen her offend some of her classmates in some of the exercises. As she approached me I could see she was not happy. But I was not deterred.

"I appreciate you sharing your story. But I want you to know I hate Gaddafi and I hate those people who supported him. And I see them walking through the halls of this hospital. But I know who they are and what they did to me and my family," she said.

She went on to share about the ways her family had suffered under the Gaddafi regime. It was abhorrent and she was incredibly justified in being angry. But beyond what she was saying, I heard her heart. I validated the loss and the importance of grieving. I encouraged her that it would take time, but that this country needed strong leaders who could move the country forward. In order to do that, they must be able to forgive and reconcile.

"Do you believe God is the Judge in Islam?" I asked.

"Yes, and Gaddafi is burning in hell," she said.

"Then why do you need to continue to carry this? As long as you continue to hold onto this, Gaddafi continues to control you from the grave," I said.

In that moment, that once brash woman immediately softened and began to cry. I reached out and gave her a hug. It was a tender moment that I will never forget. I realized that out of my personal loss, and willingness to respond in peace and love, that I had been given an incredible gift. I could both speak into people's lives on the individual human level, and challenge the world on a global policy level. It is a unique and strategic place to be. But it was

33

only because I had accepted the call to take the road less traveled. I had earned the blessing of influence and seen miracles because I had chosen the path of peace and true leadership.

Chapter 3: Gaddafi's early years

Libya before Gaddafi

Before the charismatic and idealistic Muammar Gaddafi rose to power in 1969, Libya was under centuries of foreign rule and territorial and political disputes and wars. It attracted different European superpowers due to its strategic location in the African continent. With the Mediterranean Sea to its north, the country was considered the "gateway of Africa" (Greavette, 2005). Libya was successfully dominated by the Turks, the Italians, the Germans, the French and the British before it gained its independence in 1951.

Libya is a total of 1,759,540 square kilometers of land area, making it Africa's fourth largest country and the world's fifteenth biggest nation (Greavette, 2005). It has the Mediterranean Sea to its north; the Maghreb region composed of the Arab countries Algeria, Mauritania, Morocco and Tunisia to its west, and the Mashreq region composed of Egypt and the Middle East to its east. Its history goes back to at least 8000 B.C. and is associated with the ancient Phoenicians, Greeks, Roman and Arabs.

In the 16th century, the powerful Ottoman Empire successfully conquered Libya's coastal areas but failed to extend their dominance to the Fezzan province and other areas occupied by Libyan tribes as they were met with strong resistance (Blanchard & Zanotti, 2011). By the 18th century, the provinces of Tripolitania and Cyrenaica were part of an Ottoman state under Ahmed Qaramanli and his family.

The Turks maintained their reign over the territory for more than a century through detaining vessels that passed by the Mediterranean Sea with the help of their own navy and pirates and asking those detained to pay for their freedom (Blanchard & Zanotti, 2011). This consequently led to the formation of the United States Navy as U.S. ships were constantly being ransacked in the late 1700s. The U.S. fought back with its marines mostly winning naval confrontations against Qaramanli naval personnel and pirates. The U.S. Marines' successful capture of Darnah in Libya's east in 1805 resulted in the weakening of the Qaramanli dynasty for most of the 19th century as it gradually lost its occupied Libyan territories to tribal movements (Blanchard & Zanotti, 2011).

By 1911, Italy was able to occupy Tripolitania and Cyrenaica and the Turks left. Libyan tribes and the provinces were hostile to the new foreign domination and fought with Italian troops for more than twenty years but were mostly marked by defeat, especially during World War I (Blanchard & Zanotti, 2011). In 1929, Italy's fascist leader Benito Mussolini gave the territory its official name "Libya," the term the Greeks utilized when referring to North Africa, with the exemption of Egypt (Sullivan, 2009).

By the Second World War, Libya was shared by Nazi Germany and Italy and was used to attack Egypt and the rest of North Africa which were then ruled by the Allies' Great Britain and France respectively (Blanchard & Zanotti, 2011). After the defeat of German and Italian troops in the early 1940s by Allied troops, control over Libya was divided, with the French in Fezzan, the British in Cyrenaica, and the Italians who remained in the territory after World War II in Tripolitania (Greavette, 2005). But by the year 1949, the divided territory was made into one independent state by the United Nations (Blanchard & Zanotti, 2011). The UN also urged the creation of a Libyan national assembly but was faced with difficulties due to ongoing tribal and regional wars.

Both the United States and the United Kingdom saw Libya as the key in controlling the Mediterranean region before their enemies, such as the Soviet Union, did. After World War II, the two Western superpowers built and improved airfields, ports and military bases (Greavette, 2005).

To secure the country under the influence of the West, Libya was finally made an independent state on December 24, 1951, under a federal constitutional monarchy proposed by the United Nations (Greavette, 2005). The Kingdom of Libya was entrusted to King Idris As Sanussi I who was from the Sanussi order that played an essential role in the defeat of the Axis during the Second World War through an alliance with the British, as well as being a key figure behind regional resistance of Italian rule. He was joined by a Prime Minister, a Council of Ministers, and a bicameral legislature (Blanchard & Zanotti, 2011).

King Idris was faced with a nation of extreme poverty and high illiteracy (Greavette, 2005). This made Libya rely heavily on foreign aid from the United States, Great Britain and France.

Fortunately, in 1955, oil was discovered in its dry lands. In 1959, Esso, a U.S. oil company, was able to find vast petroleum deposits in the region of Cyrenaica (Sullivan, 2009). This eventually turned Libya into a magnet for international oil companies and contractors from different parts of the globe. The country's economy rapidly developed as per capita income increased from a mere $20 to $30 per year to a staggering $2,000 per year in a span of two decades.

Despite the booming oil economy of Libya in the 1950s and 1960s, corruption was notoriously abundant in the Libyan monarchy. The country's oil revenue was plentiful but only benefited a few as most Libyans continued to live in poverty (Sullivan, 2009) while government officials lived in luxury and Western nations and international companies benefited by the billions with the exploitation of the country's "black gold." This sparked demonstrations by discontented Libyans against King Idris and his Western allies (Greavette, 2005). King Idris made matters worse for himself when he changed his government's federal system into a unitary monarchy, centralizing all the authority to the royalty instead of branching it out to provincial and local sectors for the sake of developing oil production (Blanchard & Zanotti, 2011). He also prohibited the formation of political parties and movements, forcing protesters to go underground. In addition, the U.S. and British support of Israel, the Arab world's mortal enemy, which led to the defeat of Arab forces in the 1967 Six Day War, led to the distaste of Libyans for Western existence in the country.

The bittersweet effect of the discovery of oil in Libya inspired several Libyans in their quest for economic, political and social change. This is what made and strengthened the 27-year-old Colonel Muammar Gaddafi's successful coup in 1969.

Young Gaddafi

Gaddafi was born in a small farming community outside of Sirte known as Qasr Abu Hadi. Muammar Gaddafi's (can also be spelled as Qaddafi, Gathafi or Qadhafi) actual birth date remains unknown, but most scholars believe that he was most likely born around the year 1942 in a tent situated in the harsh Libyan desert (Kushner, 2003). It was about twenty miles from Sirte, a town located on the country's southern coast (Black, 2000). He was born

37

and raised in nomadic yet modest conditions. His education and upbringing was typical for the residents of the area.

Gaddafi's parents were part of the small Qadhafa tribe (also spelled as Gaddafa or Qathathfa) which literally means "those who spit out or vomit" (Simons, 1996, p.170). His father was Mohammed Abdul Salam bin Hamed bin Mohammed, more popularly known as Abu Meniar, and his mother was Aisha al-Gaddafi. They were both herders of goats and camels (Blanchard & Zanotti, 2011). Gaddafi was the youngest child and only son, having two elder sisters. Abu Meniar died in 1978 while Aisha died in 1985.

The Bedouin group to which Gaddafi and his parents and relatives belonged was very active in fighting Italians during their rule over Libya. His father was even jailed for a short while for bravely revolting against Italy (Sullivan, 2009). According to Harvey Kushner (2003), Gaddafi's sense of pride and independence, as well as his ferocity, are the usual characteristics pinned to the Bedouins.

Despite poverty, Gaddafi's parents did everything in their power to send their son to school, as they were both illiterate. They were able to send him to a Koranic elementary school and then to a high school in the city of Sebha located in the southern province of Fezzan with their scarce savings (Simons, 1996).

During the mid-1950s, Gaddafi attended the Sebha preparatory school where he created a militant group with other like-minded students based on the principles of Egyptian president Gamal Abdel Nasser. Nasser rose to power through the use of a military takeover and Gaddafi wished to do the same. The school eventually kicked Gaddafi out based on his extreme political views.

Gaddafi's interest in politics began at the age of fifteen when he was able to listen on the radio to the speeches of Nasser, whom he later idolized deeply (Black, 2000). He admired Nasser's advocacy of uniting Arab nations together in order to reject Western capitalism and imperialism. Gaddafi memorized all of Nasser's speeches word for word and then recited them to his classmates. Through this, the young Gaddafi was able to gain followers in his high school, most notably Abu Bakr Yunis Jabir who became the armed forces' commander-in-chief, Abdel Salen Jalloud who became Gaddafi's trusted right hand, and Mustafa al-Kharoubi who became his chief of intelligence (Black, 2000). He formed his very own revolutionary cell where he practiced puritanism, demanding that his classmates should avoid drinking alcohol and other immoral acts, as well as rejecting capitalism and corruption brought about by the Libyan monarchy and the foreign companies that were abusing the country's rich oil reserves. He urged his followers to join in public protests against King Idris' reign which he organized himself, since he criticized the Libyan king's lack of assistance for Nasser and the Palestinian movement (Black, 2000). After these political activities, Gaddafi was eventually expelled in 1961.

Military years

The emergence of Gaddafi's ideology on politics deepened further when he attended Benghazi's military academy in 1961 after he was able to graduate from high school in Masurata city (Sullivan, 2009). Together with his allies from high school and his other comrades who also disliked King Idris and were unsatisfied with the conditions in Libya, Gaddafi formed the Free Officers Movement. He graduated in 1965 and was named a lieutenant and an army captain shortly after. The following year, he traveled to Great Britain and entered the Royal Armored Corps' nine-month training program (Greavette, 2005). Gaddafi's records while in training were very poor as he was often reported for his "rudeness and insubordination" (Black, 2000, 250). While in Britain, he witnessed first-hand immorality and racial and class discrimination which he believed were the evil sprouts of Westernization. This was the time when his hatred for the West grew, which inspired him to do something about it starting in Libya.

Religious influences

Gaddafi grew up as a Muslim. In fact, in his early years of recruiting for his cause, he used Islam as a motivator and encouraged his recruits to have good devout living. Yet, anyone who looked at his life would see that he did not respect the conservative values of Islam, instead choosing to live his life as he pleased, without giving account to anyone or anything. He had no values, beyond himself. You would hear in the news about his attempts to share Islam with women in Italy and building mosques in Africa. In meetings with non-Muslim leaders and guests he would always interrupt meetings

39

to pray. He even did this in the Kremlin in Russia. But it was just a façade and likely an attempt to make up for his bad deeds.

There is also evidence that Gaddafi was involved in witchcraft as was evidenced by the books on witchcraft found in his hideaway when it was raided during the revolution. There were also statements that during the revolution, Gaddafi had his soldiers wear amulets that were designed to protect and give them power. Being power hungry like most dictators, he likely looked to witchcraft to give him power to lead and an edge in overcoming his opponents. Similar witchcraft has been used by other leaders who have drawn upon the power of the dark side.

Joseph Koney is the most notable recent leader who used witchcraft. For years, it always seemed that Koney was one step ahead of authorities when they were trying to capture him. Then the Uganda government found out that Koney had developed altars around the country. When the government and church in Uganda rose up and started to pray, they got divine insight where these altars were. As they tore down the altars, Koney lost his power and quickly lost his foothold in Uganda.

Leadership Lessons

At a very early age, Gaddafi demonstrated one of the foundational attributes of leadership, vision. To have vision is to guide and motivate people with a compelling viewpoint. Gaddafi was influenced by Nasser's vision for uniting Arab nations to reject Western capitalism and what they perceived as imperialism. Young Gaddafi used Nasser's speeches to inspire and motivate his classmates to join his revolution as he presented a clear picture of where he wanted to go and how to achieve it.

For a fifteen-year-old teen to enlist people into his vision, he must have demonstrated a great deal of influence and ability to persuade people that he was credible and that he could achieve it. This was likely spurred on by his strong charisma and idealism. Many Libyans have told me that in his early days, Gaddafi was an idealist and started his revolution to improve their lives. Then he strayed far off that original path.

Chapter 4: Gaddafi's rise to power

The coup

After returning to Libya from Great Britain, Gaddafi continued his underground movement against the Libyan monarchy, molding his loyal officers to ensure that his mission to overthrow King Idris would become successful. By the year 1969, the Libyan government lost most of the Libyan people's support, putting them in a very weak and vulnerable situation, which Gaddafi and his men took advantage of. In June of 1969, the king fell ill and had to fly to Greece for an operation, leaving his nephew Prince Hasan ar-Rida in charge of Libya (Sullivan, 2009). The absence of King Idris was the perfect time for Gaddafi to act. Along with seventy other military officers, the 27-year-old Libyan soldier was able to overthrow the monarchy in a bloodless coup on September 1, 1969. They were able to occupy Tripoli, Benghazi, Zawia and other smaller Libyan cities (Greavette, 2005). The coup was easily put into play since, as Gaddafi said, "the country was up for grabs" (as quoted by Sullivan, 2009, 27) during this time. He was immediately made Libya's new leader and ruled over the country with his own kind of government, which he molded from his personal ideology, for more than forty years until his death.

Familial influences

Colonel Muammar Gaddafi had two wives, seven biological sons, one biological daughter and two adopted daughters. His first wife was Fatiha al-Nuri, to whom he was married for only a year. They only had one child, Muhammad Gaddafi, the Libyan leader's eldest son, who was born in 1970 (*Hindustan Times,* 2011). Muhammad was the former head of the Libyan Olympic Committee.

Gaddafi met his second wife, Safia Farkash, in 1969 after the successful coup when he was hospitalized for appendicitis and she was a teenage nursing student in the hospital where he was being cared for (*Hindustan Times,* 2011). They were married in 1970 following Gaddafi's divorce from his first wife. The couple had six sons and one daughter.

The Libyan leader's eldest son with Farkash is Saif Al Islam who was rumored as Gaddafi's heir by many. Born in 1972, he was educated in Great Britain and Austria and eventually became an architect (*Hindustan Times*, 2011). Like his father, Saif Al Islam was uniquely eccentric as he reportedly purchased two Bengali tigers he named Barney and Fred for $15,000 (Black, 2000). During the 2000s, he served as one of his father's most important officials, often participating in international negotiations and talks, as well as speaking on behalf of Gaddafi in the international community.

In 1973, Farkash gave birth to Gaddafi's third son, Al-Saadi. He is known for being a professional soccer player and his troublesome past while in Europe related to alcohol and drugs (*Hindustan Times*, 2011). Gaddafi's fourth son, Mutassim, born in 1974, served in the Libyan Army and was later made the country's security advisor by his father (*Hindustan Times*, 2011). Hannibal Muammar, born in 1975, is Gaddafi's most troublesome son, having been arrested several times in different countries.

Gaddafi's only daughter, Aisha, was born in 1976. She is known for being one of the defense lawyers of Iraq's Saddam Hussein during his trial that ended in his execution in 2006 (*Hindustan Times*, 2011). Aisha was also one of the United Nations' ambassadors of goodwill up until the 2011 massacres of protesting civilians in Libya.

Saif al-Arab, Gaddafi's sixth son, was born in 1982. He lived for a few years in Germany and was a businessman before serving in the Libyan army during the Libyan civil war in 2011 (*Hindustan Times*, 2011). Colonel Gaddafi's youngest son, Khamis, who was born in 1983, also served in the Libyan army.

Gaddafi and Farkash also adopted two children named Milad and Hana. There is currently very limited information on their daughter Milad and her whereabouts (*BBC News*, 2011). Hana was allegedly killed when she was sixteen months old after a U.S. air strike on Gaddafi's living quarters in Tripoli in 1986 (Greavette, 2005). But after Gaddafi's death, Libyan rebels ransacked the Libyan leader's home and found pictures of a woman named Hana who is believed to be the same Hana that the Gaddafi family claimed to have died during the 1986 air strike (*Hindustan Times*, 2011). Witnesses claim that she served as a surgeon in one of Tripoli's hospitals.

Mentors

Gaddafi's "Egyptianization of Libya" (Greavette, 2005) through the motto of his revolution, "Freedom, Socialism, and Unity," was made possible by his admiration for Gamal Abdel Nasser who led the 1952 Egyptian Revolution that successfully overthrew the Egyptian and Sudanese monarchy. Despite identifying himself with Nasser, the Libyan leader acknowledged his idol's shortcomings, especially after Nasser's humiliating defeat in the Arab-Israeli Six Day War in 1967 (Black, 2000). He tried to be better, almost godlike with his vision of a Libyan utopia.

Personality plus

In his early years, Gaddafi was very charismatic and this charisma drew loyal followers who ultimately helped him in his coup and later in leading Libya. There are likely many psychological profiles Gaddafi fit into. He most definitely fit the profile and definition of a megalomaniac. Megalomania is a psychopathological disorder characterized by delusional fantasies of power, relevance or omnipotence. Megalomania also is characterized by an inflated sense of self-esteem and overestimation by persons of their powers and beliefs. Historically it was used as an old name for narcissistic personality disorder. Unfortunately, narcissism is a very common trait of people in power. But most narcissists would not engage in the type of acts that Gaddafi did. He also was a sociopath with no conscience or moral compass who likely had manic-depressive tendencies based on his seasons of periodic withdrawal. He had many phobias like fear of tunnels, elevators and long flights.

As typical of narcissists, he was obsessed with his looks. He had plastic surgery by a Brazilian plastic surgeon to fix his receding hairline and regularly had Botox injections because he hated wrinkles. He often wore extravagant and outlandish clothes, once again always wanting to be noticed. He was most definitely noticed, but not in an admiring way, but instead as foolish, often making him the focus of political cartoons. Perhaps Gaddafi believed that old saying that all press is good press.

One of Gaddafi's interests was reading and he used it as a way to prove his intellect. He used to read a lot of military, political and civilian history books. Before visiting any state, he would get himself up to speed with its entire history throughout the trip; and when he met with the leaders of those countries, he would pick something out from their history in order to surprise them with it, sometimes things they didn't even know.

Gaddafi was an arrogant man who believed that he was the only one who knew anything and that he was an expert in law, economy and social and political affairs. "He had the first and final say in all matters and he would accept no opposition from anyone. He liked to brag and he liked whoever praised him and told him that he is the best. Anyone who complied with him would obtain many gains" (Nuri Mismari, Alhayat.com interview, July 14, 2012). He was a temperamental person and very difficult to work with. When he would receive world leaders as guests, he would insist on having his chair be taller than theirs. Yet when he would visit other countries, he did not treat other countries' leaders with the same respect. He was always scheming, wanting things his way and provoking problems with his demands, like demanding his tent be placed in the garden palaces in places like France and Russia. The French refused, but the Russian government finally agreed when they realized Gaddafi wasn't bringing a camel, but just a tent.

Gaddafi was manipulative and used to enjoy insulting other leaders. He used to run late for his appointments or suddenly modify his schedule to confuse his hosts or break protocol. He purposely annoyed his guests by giving them appointments in the desert. "He once came up with a plan to insult Kofi Annan, former Secretary General of the United Nations, who had come to discuss the Lockerbie issue. He received him at night, in the desert, in a dreadful camp" (Nuri Mismari, Alhayat.com interview, July 14, 2012). Gaddafi disrespected and spoke ill of nearly every world leader. He insisted on using the term "My Son" when addressing world leaders, including U.S. President Barack Obama. He used to say "bring me the black slave" when asking his protocol officer to bring him leaders of African nations (Nuri Mismari, Alhayat.com interview, July 14, 2012). It was his way of humiliating them. In his later years he had a good relationship with Hugo Chavez, President of Venezuela. When he visited North Korea, Kim Jong-Il received him with huge human and artistic procession, finally giving him the kind of acknowledgement as a leader that he believed he deserved.

As an Arab, he always desired to create a united Arab movement, but instead he had especially bad relations with all the Arab leaders. "He did not think Mubarak was his equal, despised both Arafat and Abbas, and he disliked Saddam because of his arrogance. There was extreme animosity between Gaddafi and Saddam and Gaddafi even supported Saddam's opponents in Iraq. Yet, he later offered asylum to Saddam, even having his daughter Aisha, who is a lawyer, serve on Saddam's defense team. He closely followed Saddam's trial fearing it would one day be his own fate" (Nuri Mismari, Alhayat.com interview, July 14, 2012).

Gaddafi plotted to have King Abdullah of Saudi Arabia assassinated because he hated him. Gaddafi's abhorrence of well-off people began during his childhood. He grew up in a very poor family with a father who was a shepherd who worked for the Wali of Fezzan, during the early period of Libyan independence. Libya was divided into three states, Tripoli, Cyrenaica and Fezzan. Gaddafi was a mischievous boy, who hated any well-off person. The father of his cousin Ahmed Gaddafi al-Dam was a lieutenant in the motorized division. They were well-off and helped Muammar's family. Muammar Gaddafi held a grudge against the wealthy, especially royal families. That coupled with Saudi Arabia's political, economic and Islamic weight made Gaddafi envious of the Saudis' power and therefore made him despise them (Nuri Mismari, Alhayat.com interview, July 14, 2012).

One Palestinian that he liked was Ahmad Jibril, a founder of the Popular Front for Liberation of Palestine-General Command. Jibril was a convicted terrorist and even one of the people initially seen as a suspect in the Lockerbie bombing. In fact, during the Lockerbie trial in the Netherlands, Jibril was subpoenaed by the prosecution to testify as to his whereabouts at the time of the bombing.

Despite his contempt and disrespect of all leaders, Gaddafi had a special relationship with former Italian Prime Minister Silvio Berlusconi. At the People's General Congress, Libya's parliament, Berlusconi shocked even Gaddafi's leaders when after giving his speech, he approached Gaddafi and kissed his hand. Yet despite this strange relationship, Gaddafi in appearance hated Italians. He was

45

always asking for compensation. Through an agreement with Berlusconi, he took with his right and gave back with his left (Nuri Mismari, Alhayat.com interview, July 14, 2012). Gaddafi would travel to Italy and have Italian women brought to him and he would lecture them about Islam while the cameras were present, trying to project an image of a good Muslim. Then later he would choose one of the women (Nuri Mismari, Alhayat.com interview, July 14, 2012).

In truth, Gaddafi hated almost everyone. He hated and cursed Islamists like Osama Bin Laden. In his early years, he used Islam as the rallying force for his supporters, but throughout the rest of his life he proved to be a bad Muslim by every definition. His behavior was in no way indicative of a devout religious Muslim. He even made it illegal for Libyans to go to mosque too many times a week, using that as a way to prevent Islamists from gaining a foothold in the country again, after he imprisoned and executed many of them who had spoken out against him.

Gaddafi was power hungry and lived in fear of his opponents. So a campaign was headed up by Abdul Salam Jalloud and later Moussa Koussa to travel to universities around the world and kidnap and assassinate Gaddafi opponents (Nuri Mismari, Alhayat.com interview, July 14, 2012).

Despite Gaddafi's disdain for most people, he often supported revolutionary causes. He respected what he considered to be "freedom fighters" or groups that he saw as such. In Iraq he supported Saddam's opponents, in Ireland he gave money to the IRA. In the U.S. he gave money to the Nation of Islam, the African-American Islamic group run by Farrakhan, and to the Native American community, both of which spoke out and supported a rally held in Gaddafi's honor which I attended the day he spoke at the United Nations. While Gaddafi was inside speaking, several thousand Nation of Islam members, Libyan students and Native Americans participated in a "pep rally" in Gaddafi's honor outside the United Nations while several other anti-Gaddafi demonstrations went on within the same vicinity. I stood in the middle of the crowd shocked at what I was watching.

"He was a coward who claimed to be brave. When we used to take part in conferences, he used to ask us to find out where the emergency exits are. He used to say, 'Put guards there. You must also have flashlights. If the lights go out, you should turn your flashlights on. Those sitting by the exits should send signals so that we know that there is a gate that we can use to leave.' He was a coward. I said that he would never leave Libya because I know he's stubborn and that he would never surrender. He cannot imagine his life without power. But this is not because he was brave. He used to take some pills that improved his morale and gave him a feeling of courage and power" (Nuri Mismari, Alhayat.com interview, July 14, 2012).

During the height of Gaddafi's tense relations with the U.S., he outlawed all English in Libya. English wasn't taught in school and all the signs on shops, buildings or street signs had to be in Arabic. Some said that he did not want the street signs in English in case there was an invasion by America, he didn't want the people to know how to get to key locations.

Gaddafi had the inability to empathize with others and when leaders declined his invite for meetings or dinners, he refused to believe it had anything to do with him, claiming instead that his staff had not delivered the invites.

Gaddafi constantly broke protocol out of a desire to embarrass people. When he spoke at the UN, he refused to wait in the on-deck waiting room, where protocol would have the speaker shake the hand of the preceding speaker and exchange pleasantries, because he followed Obama. So, instead Gaddafi went directly from his seat to the podium and intentionally spoke for 95 minutes with a diatribe against the United Nations while attempting to tear a copy of the charter. After not being able to tear it because it was too thick, he simply threw the pages in a shameful way. His behavior became the laughingstock of the United Nations that year.

Anger and abusive behavior was the norm for Gaddafi. When he got angry he would go into a tirade and often abuse his staff. If he got really angry, he sent them to jail. Most of his staff and team appeared to lead out of fear more than loyalty as was evidenced by how quickly they jumped ship and changed sides during the revolution. Some held on for a while, likely waiting to see if there was enough momentum to topple Gaddafi. But the ones who remained loyal to him in the end, likely did so out of fear their own corrupt behavior would come out. When you also have unclean hands like many of Gaddafi's advisors and thugs such as Abdullah Senussi, you aren't motivated to change.

Gaddafi was bloodthirsty, even exhibiting this by washing his hands in the warm blood of an animal he had hunted. He dealt quickly and swiftly in violence against anyone or anything that could harm him or his reputation. For example, it came out that Gaddafi's mother was Jewish through documents his advisor received from Italy. So, Gaddafi systematically killed off everyone who knew his mother was Jewish including Saleh Bou Farwa, one of the Free Officers, who was shot dead on a hunting trip in Romania, and later Amma Daou, the Libyan Ambassador to Italy, and the press secretary were also assassinated by Gaddafi, while he blamed it on Gaddafi's opponents (Nuri Mismari, Alhayat.com interview, July 14, 2012).

The wickedness of Gaddafi also extended into a deeply perverted and deviant sexually sadistic behavior. He was known to have his Amazonian Guard, a group of beautiful women that served as his personal bodyguards and his harem. But since Gaddafi's death, the truth about his deep sexual perversion has come to full light. According to his advisors he was bisexual and a pedophile. He had a group called "the services group" which was a group of boys kept for Gaddafi's pleasure (Nuri Mismari, Alhayat.com interview, July 14, 2012). He was known to rape female dignitaries both inside and outside of Libya. One account involved Gaddafi's rape and abuse of a female doctor from Nigeria who was visiting Libya. She was left bloodied, bruised, scratched, and with bite marks on her body. When confronted Gaddafi denied it and simply paid her off with $100,000 (Ibid.). Nothing was off limits for Gaddafi because he believed he could do whatever he wanted and would simply pay people off with blood money to keep their silence. Gaddafi even used to take revenge upon people with their wives.

Leadership Lessons

Any idealistic motives Muammar Gaddafi had when he originally led the revolution, were quickly disbanded. As the adage says, "Absolute power corrupts absolutely." One of the foundational leadership attributes that Gaddafi lacked was emotional intelligence. Emotional intelligence refers to the capacity to recognize your own feelings and those of others. Emotionally intelligent leaders are more likely to achieve results in their desires for change. Gaddafi's

48

lacking this key leadership attribute was likely one of the key reasons he never achieved the greatness he desired. Instead, he showed his stripes of lacking any emotional intelligence as he displayed anger and abusive behavior.

He also lacked integrity in his dealings with everyone. His inner motives were deceptive and corrupt and therefore he was untrustworthy. People followed him out of fear, not out of trust.

As a narcissist he lacked even a remnant of humility. A humble leader recognizes they are no better than the people they serve. They recognize they are not God. Gaddafi instead was arrogant and saw himself deserving of godlike treatment. Yet he also displayed insecurity, which caused him constantly to undermine other leaders in order to make himself look superior. He would intentionally try to disrespect leaders of other countries, which ended up causing him to be rejected by the Arab nations he so desperately desired to unite in his early days. This rejection just continued to cause his behavior to become worse. He was unable to empathize with the needs and concerns of others and therefore took the opposite approach. Like a spoiled child wanting to get even, he turned his sights to supporting revolutionary causes and terrorism around the world.

Another foundational leadership principle that Gaddafi lacked was fairness. Fairness has to do with dealing consistently and justly with people and checking all facts before making a judgment. Gaddafi played favorites. If people bowed into his demands and boosted his ego, he treated them well. However, if they crossed him, they would end up in prison or be punished in some other way. It was not uncommon for him to arbitrarily throw his own aides and staff into prison on his whims. He would punish dignitaries from other nations by raping or abusing their wives. Gaddafi lacked a conscience.

Chapter 5: Gaddafi's quest for more power

Muammar Gaddafi always wanted to be the leader of a great nation, which he believed was befitting of him. He had delusions of grandeur that led him down the road of all kinds of bad behavior, hoping it would gain him some notoriety. The only real notoriety he received was the title of "Mad Dog of the Middle East" given to him by Ronald Reagan. For years, people all over the world looked on at Gaddafi in dismay as he paraded around in his weird and often feminine clothes, often berating some leader in the news or giving his two cents on some world event. But because of his unwillingness to play well with the other Arab leaders, he quickly was shunned by the Arab leaders. So he switched his focus to the African Union. He looked at the continent of Africa with naiveté, thinking he could finally develop the influence he had always desired. He believed the "kings" of Africa could influence their tribes and people. He appointed Bachir Saleh, the head of his office, to request that Dr. Rafeh Al-Madani, head of the office of Africa's Kings and Sultans, declare Muammar Gaddafi the King of Africa's Kings (Nuri Mismari, Alhayat.com interview, July 14, 2012). Dr. Rafeh was embarrassed and said that the decision wasn't up to them (Ibid.). Bachir even asked for a crown. One of the kings had a gold crown that they used to declare Gaddafi King of Africa's Kings. He became a laughingstock around the world, even being poked fun at during the Arab Summit. Gaddafi's staff sent memos to the African Union, the European Union, and the United Nations telling them that Gaddafi's official title was "the Leader of the Revolution, Muammar Gaddafi, and the King of Africa's Kings" (Ibid.).

Assassination attempts on Gaddafi

Like many hated leaders, there were assassination attempts on Gaddafi's life. But he created an integrated secret police network in order to prevent these types of attacks. One assassination attempt was blamed on Bin Laden and the Islamic opposition. The perpetrators rode garbage trucks into Gaddafi's home when he was not there. The perpetrators came out without anyone seeing them, so Gaddafi believed it must have been a conspiracy by the special guard and he had all the special guard executed (Nuri Mismari, Alhayat.com interview, July 14, 2012).

Other assassination attempts included a coup attempt by Idriss Al-Shubheibi, who was killed in an air raid while attempting to flee to Egypt. There was also a coup staged by Omar al-Muheishi, a member of the Revolution Command Council. He disagreed with Gaddafi and started coordinating with military elements to topple him. Gaddafi became suspicious of Muheishi and prevented the assassination when Gaddafi was in Uganda. Muheishi fled to Morocco, but was returned as part of some type of deal, and Muheishi was shot (Nuri Mismari, Alhayat.com interview, July 14, 2012).

Another attempt was made by one of Gaddafi's relatives who was an officer in the Presidential Guard. He was gruesomely executed and his execution was videotaped as an example for others who might consider this act. The corpses of some of these people ended up hanging near Bab al-Azizia (Nuri Mismari, Alhayat.com interview, July 14, 2012).

Timeline of events: Political happenings during Gaddafi's reign

1969: Gaddafi seizes power on September 1 in a coup against King Idris.

1970: The new regime closes British and U.S. military bases in Libya.

1973: Foreign oil companies in Libya are nationalized.

1976: Gaddafi publishes his *Green Book*, which espouses a Marxist and anti-capitalist world view.

1977: Libya is renamed the "Socialist People's Libyan Arab Jamahiriya." Political power is formally vested in a network of "people's committees."

1980: Demonstrators attack U.S. embassy in Tripoli.

1981: U.S. fighter planes shoot down two Libyan jets over the Gulf of Sirte, which Libya claims as territorial waters.

April 1984: Shots fired from Libyan embassy in London kill policewoman Yvonne Fletcher, guarding demonstrators protesting against Gaddafi. Britain cuts diplomatic ties. Gaddafi says "we are sorry" for the killing in October 2009.

January 1986: U.S. President Ronald Reagan orders halt to economic and commercial relations with Libya, freezes Libyan assets in the United States.

--April: Libya is blamed for bombing a West Berlin disco used by U.S. servicemen, killing three.

--April: U.S. aircraft bomb Tripoli, Benghazi and Gaddafi's home. Libya says more than 40 people are killed, including Gaddafi's adopted baby daughter.

December 1988: Pan Am Flight 103 from London to New York is blown up over Lockerbie, Scotland, killing 270 people.

September 1989: Bomb explodes on a French UTA airliner over Niger, killing 170 people. In 1999, France convicts six Libyans in absentia, but Tripoli denies responsibility.

1992: The United Nations imposes sanctions on Libya for the Lockerbie bombing.

January 2001: Judges unanimously find Abdel Basset Al Megrahi guilty of murder and acquit Al Amin Khalifa Fhimah over the Lockerbie bombing. Megrahi is given mandatory life sentence.

September 2003: UN Security Council votes unanimously to lift sanctions imposed on Libya in 1992 after Libya accepts responsibility for the Lockerbie bombing.

-- December: Libya says it is going to abandon weapons of mass destruction programs and allow in international weapons inspectors.

January 2004: Lawmakers arrive on the first visit by a U.S. congressional delegation to Libya since Gaddafi came to power.

-- March: British Prime Minister Tony Blair meets Gaddafi.

May 2006: The United States says it will restore full diplomatic ties with Libya.

September 2008: Condoleezza Rice meets Gaddafi in Tripoli in the first visit by a U.S. secretary of state since 1953.

June 2009: Gaddafi makes a controversial first visit to former colonial power Italy. The next month Gaddafi and U.S. President Barack Obama shake hands during a G8 summit in Italy.

-- August: Megrahi is set free on compassionate grounds and arrives home to a hero's welcome. The next day, Britain condemns the celebrations in Tripoli.

February 17, 2011: Activists designate February 17 as a day of rage, a day after first riots in Benghazi.

-- February 22: A defiant Gaddafi vows to die "a martyr" in Libya and says he will crush a revolt which has seen eastern regions break free from four decades of his rule.

-- February 26: The UN Security Council imposes sanctions on Gaddafi and his family, and refers the crackdown on rebels to the International Criminal Court.

-- March 5: The rebel National Transitional Council (NTC) in Benghazi declares itself Libya's sole representative.

-- March 17: The UN Security Council votes to authorize a no-fly zone over Libya and military action to protect civilians against Gaddafi's army.

-- September 16: The UN Security Council eases sanctions on Libya and the UN General Assembly approves a request to accredit interim government envoys as Libya's sole representatives at the UN, effectively recognizing the NTC.

-- October 20: Gaddafi is captured and killed as NTC fighters take his hometown of Sirte.

Ideology and governmental structure: *The Green Book*

Since Muammar Gaddafi's successful coup in 1969, Libya had been identified solely with the Libyan leader. According to Lieutenant-Colonel Gordon Greavette (2005), "when speaking of Libya, its name and international reputation are synonymous with the name and international reputation of its leader." He was able to successfully apply his ideology and philosophy in bringing changes in the country's government, economy and society. But due to Gaddafi's poor relations with other nations, which was negatively affecting Libya, he was forced to change his ideology and method of governance a few times, making his 42-year rule over the country generally inconsistent with more downs than ups.

Gaddafi's ideology was earlier molded on that of Egypt's Nasser, with regards to the importance of revolution and the unification and regaining the glory of the Arab world. He raised the flag of Arab socialism, as well as Islamic nationalism. Through this, he was able to overthrow King Idris and the Libyan monarchy and transform the country "from a conservative, colonial state into a modern and progressive one" (Black, 2000, 250). But after decades in power, the charismatic, idiosyncratic Gaddafi practiced contradictory leadership and made controversial changes in his ideology, shifting from one to another depending on the Libyan conditions at hand and based on his whims.

Right after the 1969 coup, he formed the Revolutionary Command Council (RCC), composed of a twelve-member directorate, as the acting authority in Libya, of which he was the Chairman. The RCC's first task was to eliminate corruption and all signs of Western imperialism in the country (Black, 2000). They were able to completely remove all military bases of the United States, Great Britain and France in the country in the early 1970s (Kushner, 2003). In March 1970, the British left their bases in El-aden and Tobruk and a few months later, the Americans abandoned their airbase in Wheelus Airfield, emphasizing that the future of the oil industry was more essential than having military bases in the Mediterranean region (Blanchard & Zanotti, 2011).

In line with Gaddafi's vision of "Arab nationalism, Arab socialism, and Arab unity" (Greavette, 2005), as well as his goal of making Libya independent from Western capitalism and imperialism, the Libyan leader brought several economic and social changes in Libya during the first years of his regime. Gaddafi and the RCC imposed restrictions on using alcohol and other actions that were perceived by Gaddafi as sinful and against the virtues of Islam. Yet, some of Gaddafi's ambassadors confessed that they would buy their alcohol from the foreign embassies. The RCC screened and removed all corrupt government officials and military personnel from their positions, and some of them were even jailed. For Libyans, Gaddafi provided most with sources of income, free education, housing, transportation and health care, as well as abolishing the wage system and the employer-employee system (Greavette, 2005). All of these were accomplished in just a decade, which led to rapid changes and development of Libya's economy. By 1979, the Mediterranean country rich in oil had the highest GDP and GNP in the whole African continent, even beating the per capita income of Japan, the UK and Italy. Some supported Gaddafi because he began to improve their lives after centuries of discrimination, oppression and poverty under foreign rule.

Muammar Gaddafi first published the three-volume self-authored book entitled *The Green Book* in 1975 (Blanchard & Zanotti, 2011). It stood as the summation of Gaddafi's dream for Libya and the Arab world. He proposed his very own "Third Universal Theory" that was, according to him, "a practical approach to direct democracy" (Gaddafi, 1988, 7). Gaddafi believed that direct democracy is the ideal form of government and the ultimate solution to corruption and other political evils that will pave the way to economic development and social change. The Third Universal Theory is socialist in nature and is supposed to be an alternative to both capitalism and communism (Blanchard & Zanotti, 2011).

Gaddafi's *Green Book* also proposed the decentralization of political power to local committees organized by the Libyan people and urged a more proper distribution of the country's oil wealth and land.

Gaddafi's *Green Book* is composed of three sections. Its first section discussed "true" democracy as the authority of the people to lead the nation. He rejected the parliamentary form of governance, arguing that it was a "misinterpretation of the people" (Gaddafi, 1988, 2) that gave birth to "the most tyrannical dictatorships the world has known" (3). The Libyan leader was obviously referring to the most powerful of Western nations as he believed that they were the true terrorists.

The *Green Book's* first section also mentioned Gaddafi's depiction of political parties as a hindrance to unity. He claimed that the presence of multiple parties would worsen power struggles and he eventually prohibited the formation of such parties (Gaddafi, 1988). Gaddafi also made the same argument on the existence of social class systems. He added that in a true democracy, "there can be no justification for any one class to subdue other classes for its interests … no party, tribe or sect can crush others for their own interests" (5). That is why most of the Gaddafi regime's political enemies for forty years who formed groups and movements were regarded as criminals by the state and were usually jailed. The Libyan leader (1988) generally argued that:

> *"All political systems in the world today are a product of the struggle for the power between alternative instruments of government. This struggle may be peaceful or armed, as is evidenced among classes, sects, tribes, parties or individuals. The outcome is always the victory of a particular governing structure – be it that of an individual, group, party, class – and the defeat of the people; the defeat of genuine policy"* (1).

Gaddafi mentioned his strong objection to plebiscites or referendums, which he claimed are against the essence of democracy and suppress the free will of the people. He suggested the alternative of having Popular Conferences, People's Committees and the

General People's Congress, which he applied in Libya, as democracy should always be "the supervision of the people by the people" (Gaddafi, 1988, 11). Gaddafi also rejected the creation of constitutions and laws by the state. The law of society should be only about the natural laws based on a culture or religion. That is why he made the Islamic faith's holy book the Koran the constitutional law for Libya (Greavette, 2005). Gaddafi emphasized during his reign the revival of Islamdom in the place of Westernization. With the question of what happens if there are deviations to the laws in such a society, the *Green Book* suggests that will be up to the Basic Popular Conferences and People's Committees to act on these deviations and punish whoever committed them.

As for the freedom of expression, Gaddafi mentioned in his book that the press and the media should not be privately owned by individuals or companies and instead be a matter of public ownership (Gaddafi, 2005). This covered TV, radio, newspapers and book publications. In reality, Gaddafi was threatened by the agenda-setting effect and the influence media usually has on the people. Media had the power to end regimes.

In the second section of the *Green Book*, Gaddafi discussed the Third Universal Theory's economic basis. Since he focused on socialism and rejected capitalism and communism, Gaddafi (1988) believed that the ultimate solution to poverty, unequal distribution of wealth, unemployment and other economic problems all nations face was:

> "...abolishing the wage-system, emancipating people from its bondage and reverting to the natural laws which defined relationships before the emergence of classes, forms of governments and man-made laws" (13).

For every Libyan's basic source of income, Gaddafi believed that it should not be about wages acquired from anyone else in exchange for labor or services. He instead wanted the people to become "partners" (Gaddafi, 1988, 15), managing and securing their own income by their own means. Gaddafi provided Libyans in the first decade of his reign with the means of doing so, such as land, livestock and capital. Land was definitely the most essential element in an individual's "self-employment." He also encouraged doing public service in exchange for one's needs.

For housing, he rejected renting and wanted everyone to have his or her own home (Gaddafi, 1988), which he tried to do in reality by giving out free homes to homeless Libyans. This also was the case with transportation.

In addition, Gaddafi also rejected the occupation of domestic servants as "immoral" as they are removed of their freedom like slaves (Gaddafi, 1988). He believed that every person should be independent and able to support themselves by their own means, not by receiving their income from others.

The *Green Book*'s last section explained the social basis of Gaddafi's Third Universal Theory which focused on the importance of unity and a social bond in the survival of a nation (Gaddafi, 1988). The Libyan leader emphasized that the family was society's most important unit that makes up every type of groups, classes and sects. It is followed by the tribe which he considered a larger form of family. Libya is known for its indigenous tribes like the Qathathfa, Warfala and the Magharha (Black, 2000). These tribes primarily shape its government and society. Gaddafi himself was a member of the Qathathfa tribe and realized the importance of gaining the support of these Libyan tribes to his regime's survival. In addition, he noted that the tribe was "a natural social umbrella for social security" (Gaddafi, 1988, 22) while the nation was the "individual's national political umbrella" (23). Gaddafi explained that a nation is like a family or a tribe where the social bond is the center and what keeps things going, mentioning that:

> *"The nation is also a social structure whose bond is nationalism; the tribe is a social structure whose band is tribalism; the family is a social structure whose bond is family ties; and global society is a social structure whose bond is humanity"* (23-24).

In addition, Gaddafi placed a big importance on economy, military and religion in the survival of a nation, factors which he evidently valued in leading Libya. He also cited the deadly and disastrous consequences of racial and religious diversity, arguing that this could bring violent power struggles, severe discrimination, social chaos and bloody civil wars (Gaddafi, 1988). In line with this, he strongly stated that "Black people will prevail in the world" (29). Gaddafi wanted to strengthen the blacks and to overpower the white dominance. He achieved the first one with his later pan-African movement but failed miserably with the second, putting Libya in isolation and an economic downfall with his decisions and actions aiming to somehow defeat the Western superpowers.

The Libyan leader also mentioned in his book the importance of minorities to the state and that they should be given equal rights like that of the majority. Speaking of equality, Gaddafi stated that men and women are equal, but differ with regards to their respective duties in society (Gaddafi, 1988). This was because of the different biological make-up of females and males, which means that "a woman, whose created nature has assigned to her a natural role different from that of man, must be in an appropriate position to perform her natural role" (26). Gaddafi did not object to women working, just as long as they chose professions based on their biological capacity instead of changing gender roles. It's curious that he would state this but still have his Amazonian guard. The Libyan leader (1988) also strongly rejected the capitalist and the communist viewpoint on women as these types of nations maintained a low regard for the female movement despite the more modern, liberal society individuals generally live in, by emphasizing that:

> *"All societies today look upon women as little more than commodities. The East regards her as a commodity to be bought and sold, while the West does not recognize her femininity"* (28).

The *Green Book*'s last pages discussed Gaddafi's view on education, music, the arts, cinema, the theater and sports. He disliked standardization and state control over education, which is the usual case in countries, and suggested that the society itself should be the one to provide education to its members (Gaddafi, 1988). Gaddafi also wanted education to become a matter of one's choice and liking, urging the society to provide different kinds of education and give the individual the right to freely choose his or her subjects.

In music and the arts, Gaddafi urged individuals and the

society to express themselves through these norms by making use of the language one speaks spontaneously and adapting traditional or inherited practices (Gaddafi, 1988). Despite this provision, the arts were suppressed under Gaddafi. In addition, he discouraged the embrace and patronization of foreign music and art forms.

As for cinema and the theater, Gaddafi viewed individuals who attended them as people who were unsatisfied and didn't know how to live their lives, arguing that "those who direct the course of life for themselves have no need to watch life working through actors" (Gaddafi, 1988, 33). He also regarded moviegoers as illiterate. He added that Bedouins are productive and serious individuals who had no need for theaters and cinemas to entertain them as they take pleasure in simpler, more traditional forms that are spontaneous rather than predictable and acted out on stage (Gaddafi, 1988).

Sports were highly valued by Gaddafi in the *Green Book* and in reality, he had a passion for sports himself which he shared with his sons. He identified the value of sporty activities with that of eating, experiencing positive emotions such as coolness or warmth, and most especially praying (Gaddafi, 1988). The Colonel also noted the difference between private and public sports where the private type "concerns the individuals themselves" while the public type is "of concern to all people" (31). He saw the value of physical activity as beneficial to one's health, as well as its positive recreational aspect.

Muammar Gaddafi's *Green Book* was the Libyan leader's guide in governing Libya through the RCC. In 1973, he established his Cultural Revolution (Black, 2000, 250) after being displeased with the conservative and "ignorant" attitude and outlook of most Libyans. This revolution involved the replacement of the country's government with that of Gaddafi's Third Universal Theory where Arab and Islamic unity and development, direct democracy and socialism dominated over capitalism and communism.

In 1977, he declared the new Libya under the name "Great Socialist People's Libyan Arab Jamahiriya" and regarded himself as the "Leader of the Revolution" (Greavette, 2005). Jamahiriya was the term given by Gaddafi to refer to "the state of the masses" (Kushner, 2003). He regarded himself as simply "the Leader" and claimed that he was not Libya's actual head of state as power over the country was given to the people through a chain of people's committees and congresses (Black, 2000). Ministers and high-ranking officials were said to report not to him but to the people.

Libya was established by Gaddafi as the "authority of the people" with the decentralization of power and control to local people's committees and congresses (Greavette, 2005). The process of such a unique form of government starts "at the local level, [where] citizens meet in Basic People's Congresses to appoint representatives to regional and ultimately the national General People's Congress" (Blanchard & Zanotti, 2011, 18). Gaddafi's government strongly encouraged Libyans' active participation in such meetings. Despite this, turnouts were always low. The people of Libya considered the *Green Book* and the supposed governmental structure as a joke. They knew who really was in control.

The General People's Congress, which was at the top of the hierarchy of the Libyan people's congresses, was composed of twelve committee secretaries that functioned in different aspects of Libyan society, like that of cabinets in a more common form of government. But by 2000, Gaddafi decided to remove these twelve and made them provincial (Blanchard & Zanotti, 2011).

Despite the supposed decentralized state of Libya's government under Colonel Gaddafi, most of the country's most important sectors were under the centralized General People's Committee. It controlled Libya's finance, foreign affairs, justice and security (Blanchard & Zanotti, 2011), which made outsiders question the trueness of Gaddafi's good intentions in decentralizing his government supposedly for the people to rule over the country. In the late 2000s, the replacement and reshuffling of secretaries and other officials of the Congress occurred.

This form of government, architected by Gaddafi himself, lasted until his death in 2011 and failed miserably as years went by. More and more Libyans grew discontent and opposed Gaddafi's authoritarian-like influence over the people's committees and congresses. In 2008, out of desperation to somehow win the citizens over, Gaddafi proposed abolishing most of the administrative sectors of Libya's government and paying out the country's oil revenues to every Libyan citizen monthly through a Wealth Distribution Program (Blanchard & Zanotti, 2011). It never pushed through.

Gaddafi's Libya was heavily backed up by a tight security

force and intricate secret police network composed of military elites, private guards and some People's Committees from the various regions and localities (Black, 2000). This made it impossible for Gaddafi's critics, most notably the Muslim Brotherhood or others that had good intentions and methods of resistance (Blanchard & Zanotti, 2011), to make a move, or to just simply rally peacefully in the streets. Violence, torture and even murder were often associated with the Libyan leader's security personnel.

The Libyan leader's inner circle and Libya's chain of command changed several times in a span of forty years until his death. They were composed of Gaddafi's revolutionary companions he met while attending secondary school and the military academy and loyal followers who had been supporting him since day one (Black, 2000). The actual hierarchy of his circle was characterized as confusing and vague, often rumored to be on purpose.

Every powerful leader in history and in modern times always has his right hand, his wingman. Since the successful revolution in 1969 that overthrew Libya's monarchy, Colonel Muammar Gaddafi's closest ally was Abdel Salen Jalloud, whom he first met while attending secondary school in Sebha (Simons, 1996). Jalloud belonged to the Magharha tribe, a rival of the Qathathfa that Gaddafi was part of. Their friendship gradually fell apart and Jalloud was eventually replaced by someone else. Speculations spread that Gaddafi felt threatened due to the growing surmises that his former number two man would most likely replace him as Libya's leader. Abdallah al-Senussi, Gaddafi's wife's brother-in-law, was then given Jalloud's position (Black, 2000). He was also a member of the Magharha and was suspected of doing the Libyan leader's "dirty jobs." In the late 1990s, al-Senussi was convicted by a French court for his involvement in the UTA DC-10 bombing in Niger in 1989 (Black, 2000). After his conviction, he was rarely with Gaddafi and in public.

Gaddafi's chaotic inner circle gradually diminished after the revolution and the creation of the RCC. It seemed that the Colonel eventually developed a distrust for his longest and closest comrades, often seeing them as a threat after he himself put them in a high position in Libya's government (Black, 2000), which was quite contradictory. Gaddafi's exclusive inner circle was like a beautiful flame and individuals who wanted to get in were moths attracted to the flame, waiting to get themselves burnt and killed.

Gaddafi's regime was centered on Libyan tribes as most of the Libyan leader's officials were of tribe membership. They existed way before foreign colonialists came to the country. They remain and most of them dominate the politics and armed forces of Libya.

Gaddafi, a Qathathfa member, maintained and emphasized the importance of tribes during his regime. He knew that gaining the support and loyalty of these tribes were extremely essential in his security and most importantly his longevity and survival in his Libyan throne. Gaddafi gave several members of Qathathfa high-ranking positions in the government and the military (Blanchard & Zanotti, 2011). He entered Qathathfa junior officers to Libya's armed forces and air force, and assigned them to very important posts. Among them were Masoud Abdul-Hafith, the commander of military security; Khalifa Ihneish, the commander of armaments and munitions; Omar Ishkal and Al-Barani Ishkal, the commanders of domestic security, and Ali al-Kilbo, the commander of the Azziziya barracks who was responsible for the security of the Libyan leader's private residence (Black, 2000). Aside from the military sectors, several Qathathfa members were also behind the most significant national and regional positions and cabinets in Libya. The region of Cyrenaica was tasked with Ahmad Qathf al-Damm while Benghazi was supervised by Misbah Abdul-Hafith (Black, 2000). One of Gaddafi's relatives, Mohamad al-Majthoub Gaddafi, was given the position as the leader of the revolutionary committees.

Despite Gaddafi's obvious bias to his own tribe where government and military positions were concerned, he recruited several members of the Magharha tribe in his inner circle, most notably his former right hands Abdel Salen Jalloud and Abdallah al-Senussi (Black, 2000). The members of the large Warfalla tribe, Qathathfa's rival, were given small positions in Gaddafi's regime on the other hand. This led to Warfalla opposition groups accusing the Colonel of tribal discrimination (Blanchard & Zanotti, 2011). Several coup attempts were carried out by his very own military all throughout his regime due to such rivalries over tribal domination. Gaddafi tried to prevent these military coups from being successful by reassignment and extermination of officers and soldiers who were possible catalysts to such opposition (Blanchard & Zanotti, 2011). This strategy instead worsened the Libyan military's incapability and

63

incompetence in securing the safety of Gaddafi's Libya and its citizens.

Libya's media was heavily controlled by Gaddafi, having numerous restrictions on what to say, write and publish via different media channels (Sullivan, 2009). But when it came to gaining international attention and satisfying his vanity for his work of art which was Libya, the Libyan leader usually opened his doors to journalists and public figures from Western and African nations (Black, 2000). He was often viewed by outsiders as highly eccentric, which was exactly what made him newsworthy for many. When being interviewed, Gaddafi would always prefer being "in a camel-skin tent, attired in a Bedouin robe over Western-style casual wear" (Black, 2000, 253). Through this, he wanted to portray himself as being a simple-living leader who embraced traditional Bedouin ways when in fact he was notoriously known for his unusually luxurious lifestyle and purchases.

In relation to Gaddafi's idiosyncrasy, the Libyan leader used to release a new set of rules and regulations every year on what Libyans should wear (Black, 2000). He also made such controversial policies on what they should say or write, in line with Gaddafi's control over the press. He even controlled their eating habits, giving out official lists of what and what not to eat.

Since Gaddafi urged that every citizen should be self-sufficient in terms of acquiring income (Gaddafi, 1988), he made several domestic policies for the Libyans to follow. In 1977, he argued that "in order to achieve self-sufficiency, every Libyan family had to raise chickens in home" (Black, 2000, 254). The Libyan government then required every household to own chickens. Libyans were asked to pay $57 each for imported cages that were solely distributed by the government (Black, 2000). This was met with utmost criticism in terms of its significance in making a living and its practicality, especially in the cities and urban areas. Most Libyans could only afford to live in apartments that were highly unfit places to raise livestock.

Gaddafi made other utterly unusual policies throughout his ever-changing way of thinking during his reign. He replaced the Gregorian calendar with the Lunar Islamic calendar used by most Muslim nations. This type of calendar began with the migration of the Islamic religion's Prophet Mohammed in the year 622 (Black,

2000). Gaddafi changed and invented the names of every month himself. Shortly after, he decided to make a change in the Lunar Islamic calendar that was one of a kind. He designed a calendar that started with Mohammed's death instead of his migration (Black, 2000). This caused great confusion to most Libyans and outsiders who visited the country, often not knowing what the actual date was.

Colonel Muammar Gaddafi's greatest architecture that was Libya was molded by his contradictory ideologies and beliefs that always seemed to change depending on the Libyan leader's mood and the condition of his country. These changes caused his downfall instead of ensuring the survival of his regime.

Impact of oil wealth

The discovery of oil in 1955 and the introduction of foreign oil companies in 1959 spurred the rapid growth and development of Libya's economy. When King Idris became the country's leader, he was left with a highly impoverished nation. Libya seemed to largely depend on foreign aid during that time rather than its rich oil reserves that seemed to only make foreign investors rich (Blanchard & Zanotti, 2011). Excessive corruption within the monarchy also made matters worse as Libyans grew discontented and angry with the lack of actual good changes and conditions in the country. The "Western Powers were happy" (Greavette, 2005) along with their Libyan monarchy back-up, while most of Libya's citizens remained poor until Muammar Gaddafi came into the picture.

The greed for oil that was behind Libya's suffering inspired Gaddafi to transform the country and the way the government functioned. Immediately after he made himself "the Leader," he concentrated on nationalizing the oil industry and properly allocating oil revenues (Blanchard & Zanotti, 2011). The Libyan government under Gaddafi monopolized oil distribution, making it the country's biggest industry and source of income. He used the power of oil to remove foreign military bases in the country and force Western nations to not intervene in Libya's matters in his first decade of his regime. During his years of support of terrorism and the development of Libya's own weapons of mass destruction (WMD), Gaddafi made use of billions of dollars of oil revenues to finance different terrorist groups in different parts of the world and to provide for the country's nuclear, biological and chemical weapons programs (Black, 2000). He also utilized Libya's large petrodollars in gaining favors from the different tribes and discouraging the formation of opposition groups that could remove him from power.

Libya's discovered oil reserves totaled 43.7 billion barrels in 2011, making it the ninth biggest oil producer in the world (Blanchard & Zanotti, 2011). More of Libya's land has yet to be explored for "black gold." Since the 1950s, Western oil companies have been trying to gain profit from the Mediterranean nation's oil by investing on oil exploration and production. To monitor the proper handling of negotiations and agreement with these foreign companies, the 1955 oil law was passed and the Libyan National Oil Company (NOC) was given the task to make sure that this law was being followed (Blanchard & Zanotti, 2011). It supervised production activities of oil reserves and gave restrictions to foreign investors.

With oil being "the lifeblood of the Libyan economy and government" (Blanchard & Zanotti, 2011, 25) since the early 1960s, the country's economy fluctuated with its high and lows as global oil prices change all the time. Aside from fluctuating oil prices, the international sanctions given to Libya by the United States and other Western countries, as well as the United Nations in the 1980s under the Iran-Libya Sanctions Act (ILSA) left the country's oil industry in ruins (Donnelly & Serchuk, 2004). By the 1990s, Libya was completely isolated from the oil market, causing a rapid decline in the country's productivity and advancement. Since Gaddafi was running out of money to feed his followers and his people, a number of groups that were against his regime emerged (Black, 2000). Yet the Libyan leader continued to spend Libya's money wastefully on out-of-this-world projects. One of these was his plan for a drastic makeover in the Sahara's landscape with the "Great Man-Made River Project" that was worth $25 billion and never even completed (Black, 2000). Corruption was also rampant during this time, especially in the localities.

Fortunately, Gaddafi decided to negotiate with the United States and other enemy countries. In the 2000s, Libya was slowly able to make amends with its former enemies which eventually led to the removal of sanctions (Donnelly & Serchuk, 2004). Foreign investments began to flow back and Libya's economy started to improve. To further improve oil productivity and exploration, the government established a Council for Oil and Gas Affairs in 2006 (Blanchard & Zanotti, 2011). Libya exported its billions of barrels of oil to the United States, France, Germany, Italy and Spain. In the United States alone, Libya was able to export up to 102,000 barrels per day in the late 2000s before Gaddafi's fall in 2011 (Blanchard & Zanotti). Despite these improvements in the oil economy of Libya, oil production has declined to half in the past decade. That is why Gaddafi and his government planned on attracting more foreign investments starting in 2005, but they failed to do so after several complications in the United States and Libya's supposed improving relations and the 2011 Libyan civil war.

Aside from oil, Libya is also rich in natural gas. Its discovered natural gas reserves are measured to be about 54 trillion cubic feet but most areas in the country remained generally remain unexplored and unprofitable because of international sanctions and investment restrictions by the Gaddafi regime (Blanchard & Zanotti, 2011). Despite this, Libya managed to be able to utilize its natural gas in power generation, as well as export it to limited number of European nations. After international sanctions were finally removed and Gaddafi started making amends for his past terrorist activities, more and more foreign companies became interested in natural gas exploration and export in Libya. In 2007, British Petroleum (BP) signed an agreement with Libya to be able to explore and export its plentiful reserves (Blanchard & Zanotti, 2011). In 2008, the Russian company Gazprom developed an interest in buying the country's natural gas and helping out the government in building new pipelines that extend to Europe (Blanchard & Zanotti, 2011). And in early 2011, despite the growing tensions between the Gaddafi regime and Libyan opposition groups, one of the biggest oil companies in the world, Shell, continued to explore Libyan territories for natural gas deposits and promised to develop the Marsa al Brega plant that has been poorly managed and maintained.

From idealism to corruption

One of my favorite sayings is that absolute power corrupts absolutely. Many Libyans would say that when Gaddafi started his leadership, he was fueled by idealism. The young Muammar Gaddafi dreamed of Arab unity and of confronting injustice and exploitation. He wanted to create a socialist nation where everyone was treated equally. In fact the roots of his idealism can be seen throughout the *Green Book*, which talks of an extreme utopian democracy. Unfortunately, what happened in Libya was quite different than what he originally hoped for. He created a dictatorship and became increasingly hungry for more and more power. The way to control the people was through systematic abuse, and oppression. The people had no voice, or influence, instead being subject to every whim of the Leader. Gaddafi had the capacity through Libya's oil wealth to make the country into a great nation. But he feared anyone or anything being more important or influential than him. So, rather than encouraging and supporting development, he held the Libyan people down. It was all about him and his power and influence. Soon, his children took on much of their father's persona, engaging in their own corrupt and abusive escapades. His children controlled the money and did everything they wished. The people of Libya had no choice but to live under that abuse and just make every effort to survive. Many Libyans began to realize the only way to get ahead was to also be corrupt. And so, a culture of corruption was born. Stealing, distrust, spying on your neighbors was the norm. No business could keep any supplies and infrastructure was allowed to deteriorate. Benghazi especially suffered under Gaddafi's reign, because they were considered the intellectual capital of Libya and home to many outspoken opponents of Gaddafi. Because of their "bad behavior" they were punished and did not receive even the minimum services that the rest of the country received. Corruption, rapes and other abuses were common among everyone in leadership positions during the regime. Managers were put into positions of authority based on loyalty to Gaddafi and not on any qualifications or skill set. This incompetence just added to the lack of structure or efficiency in any service area. There were no systems and no reason for people to be motivated to do good, improve themselves or help out. It was each person for himself or herself. The only loyalty and trust was within families. Being a socialist nation, everyone got the same amount of money whether they worked hard or not at all. People could not be fired, and no one ever received feedback on how to improve. So, as Gaddafi planned the country lay stagnant.

Leadership Lessons

Leaders know how to delegate and empower the people they serve. Delegation is about decentralizing control and empowerment is equipping the people with the skills and resources they need to be successful. In theory, Gaddafi's governmental structure was the Jamahriya, "state of the masses," which put control in the hands of the Libyan people and their local committees. Yet, in practice that was often not the case. *The Green Book* was a very idealistic book that could have empowered the people to live good, almost utopian existences. Yet, in truth Gaddafi and his arbitrary policies prevented any true level of empowerment. Instead, Gaddafi intentionally held down the Libyan people through systematic oppression. This included an intricate secret police network that would monitor all areas of people's lives. He regulated all areas of their lives, provided no capacity-building programs and intentionally allowed infrastructures to fall into disrepair when the people in different areas were not complicit with him.

Gaddafi also lacked any level of magnanimity, which helps to inspire trust. Magnanimity is the principle of giving credit where credit is due. A good leader takes responsibility for failures, which helps to draw the people closer together. Instead of this principle, Gaddafi blamed everyone else for the problems and gave no one credit for the good things.

Chapter 6: Gaddafi's leadership style

In theory, Libya was a country controlled by the people, the Jamahriya or state of the masses. But in truth, there was no empowerment. Everyone knew Gaddafi was in control. Anyone who wanted to live, did what he said or faced the consequences. People were not valued, and their voices were not heard. Instead, they just lived in a place of oppression and fear, while doing their best to live the best life they could. The best analogy is they lived like children in an abusive home. You learn to cope, do your best to not provoke your abusive parent, avoid him whenever possible, learn to play the game and keep him happy, while every day praying for the moment you can break free and find a better life.

Unlike good leaders, there was no trust of the people for Gaddafi and his cronies. Instead, they followed out of fear. Those who tried to break free of his control or revolt were made examples of. They were imprisoned, beaten and executed. Even those Libyans who managed to leave the country for education in other countries, were hunted down and kidnapped when there were rumors of them speaking out against Gaddafi and his regime. Many who opposed Gaddafi disappeared never to return again. Some of Gaddafi's leaders followed in his steps, using abuse and corruption to control the people while making a good life for themselves. It was the way things were done. Other of Gaddafi's key advisors fled into exile when it was clear the direction Gaddafi was going. The lucky ones are the ones who were able to obtain citizenship status in other countries and begin a new life. But even those who got away, kept very quiet about Libya, what they knew, and what people's lives were like, because of fear.

Human rights record

Libya in the 1900s was surrounded by violence and killings of citizens caught up in the war. By the 1950s when it regained its freedom from foreign rule, its human rights condition improved. When Gaddafi took over in 1969, peace was generally observed. But as years passed, violence and injustice resurfaced in Libyan society as Gaddafi's regime was faced with strong opposition, causing the Colonel and his officials to handle matters with an iron fist. The armed forces under Gaddafi were known as brutal and were suspected of torture, unjust imprisonments and killings of members of the opposition (Black, 2000). This went on until the 2000s when Gaddafi decided to improve Libya's human rights condition, in line with the country's improving relations with the United States and other nations. In 2003, Colonel Gaddafi and his son Saif Al Islam Gaddafi, who was very active in his father's affairs since the turn of the 21st century, gave public speeches that they would do everything to change the reputation of Libya when it came to the practice of human rights (Blanchard & Zanotti, 2011). The "revolutionary courts" and "people's courts" that were notoriously known for violations against the human rights of Libya's citizens were removed from power. Gaddafi also tried to improve the rights and protections of Libyans from any form of injustice. Despite these efforts, Gaddafi's critics believed that these were just the measures taken by his government in order to save face, that these were "meant to support the government's efforts to improve its domestic legitimacy and international standing" (Blanchard & Zanotti, 2011, 22). In 2009, Libya's human rights had improved but not to the level of what Gaddafi had promised.

Despite Libya's restrictions, when it came to the establishment of human rights organizations in the country, Gaddafi allowed several international organizations like Amnesty International and Human Rights Watch to visit and observe Libya for the first time in 2004 (Blanchard & Zanotti, 2011). Their reports on Libya's human rights conditions were generally quite negative, as Gaddafi and his officials remained unmoved to make certain reforms, specifically on the formation and membership in groups and organizations and on the freedom of expression. Saif Al Islam, on the other hand, pushed for human rights reforms, thus the creation of the Human Rights Society, which was funded and supervised by the Gaddafi Development Foundation (Blanchard & Zanotti, 2011). This resulted in a more positive outlook toward Libya for a short while before the relationship of the United States and Libya started to fall out.

Fathi al Jahmi was a Libyan known for his outspoken advocacy for change in his country under Muammar Gaddafi. He was active in publicly criticizing the Libyan leader's regime and demanding elections and press reforms. Due to his growing influence and appeal to many Libyans, he was imprisoned in 2002 but was then released in 2004 when the United States-Libya relationship was at its peak (Blanchard & Zanotti, 2011). The Libyan government was even praised by then U.S. President George W. Bush because of this release. But al Jahmi was eventually arrested again as he never gave up voicing his opinions and urging economic, political and social change through the streets and the press. Tensions started to form between the U.S. and Libya when the government denied the release of al Jahmi despite the Bush administration's intervention (Blanchard & Zanotti, 2011). This remained the case until Barack Obama became the U.S. president in 2009.

Despite the Libyan government's efforts to improve its human rights conditions, a U.S. Department State report (2010) found that the country's human rights still remained very poor:

> "...continuing problems included reported disappearance; torture; arbitrary arrest; lengthy pretrial and sometimes incommunicado detention; official impunity; and poor prison conditions. Denial of fair public trial by an independent judiciary, political prisoners and detainees, and the lack of judicial recourse of alleged human rights violations were also problems" (as quoted by Blanchard & Zanotti, 2011, 22).

Obama's administration demanded the release of the political prisoner al Jahmi on the grounds of his poor health condition while in prison. He was eventually freed and was put in the custody of Jordan until his untimely death in May 2009 (Blanchard & Zanotti, 2011). This worsened the growing conflict within the U.S.-Libya relationship. And in 2011, matters worsened for Gaddafi with a series of massacres of protesting civilians by the Colonel's men (*BBC News*, 2011). It erased all the respect and acceptance the international community had for Gaddafi and his government.

Since the Libyan revolution, more information has come out about Gaddafi's human rights abuses. One of the most noteworthy is the day after the fourth anniversary of the Lockerbie bombing, a Libyan Arab Airlines Boeing 727 disintegrated on its approach to

Tripoli airport, claiming the lives of all 157 passengers and crew. The crash, on December 22, 1992, was blamed on a midair collision with a Libyan MiG 23 fighter jet. The flight numbers were eerily similar. The airliner was flight 1103 - Pan AM flight 103 blew up over Lockerbie in southern Scotland in 1988.

The MiG's military pilot and his instructor, Majid Tayari, were sent to prison. Tayari spent 42 months behind bars for a crime he did not commit. They were too afraid to tell their side of the story when Gaddafi was in power but that has changed following the Libyan revolution, and after 20 years of silence, Tayari is determined to prove he was not responsible for the disaster. He said there was no air collision. "We were too close to each other, yes. But there was no air collision" (Tripoli Post, April 1, 2013). The air safety manager with Libyan Arab Airlines in 1992, Mahmud Tekalli, is also sure a midair collision was not the cause, and believes Flight 1103 was deliberately destroyed. "The airplane exploded in mid-air due to explosive devices, possibly put by Gaddafi agents," said Tekalli (Tripoli Post, April 1, 2013). The victims' relatives also believe the former Libyan dictator was responsible. They are convinced he wanted the 727 to blow up over the Mediterranean so that he could accuse the U.S. Navy of a revenge attack for Lockerbie (Tripoli Post, April 1, 2013).

Ruling by fear

Gaddafi was known for his tyrannical rule that left thousands of people homeless, tortured or dead. In the '70s, Gaddafi forced the exile of all ethnic Italians. Later, he forced out all of the Jewish population as well. By definition a tyranny is a cruel and oppressive governmental structure where the leader engages in use of arbitrary power and control. The atrocities of Gaddafi don't end with the exiles of Italians and Jews. He was known to severely punish anyone who was against him or had different political views. He would even order the executions of political dissidents and execute them live on public television. People who tried to flee the country to escape his tyrannical rule found themselves tracked by assassins hired by Gaddafi.

On my first trip to Libya in 2004, I was struck immediately by the overwhelming sense of oppression. From the minute I got off the plane in Tripoli, I was being observed very closely. It was said that Libya was known for having one of the most intricate secret police networks. When I walked into the hotel lobby I felt like I was walking into a bad movie set about the KGB in communist Russia. The lobby was filled with smoke and the couches were each filled with a seedy-looking man who looked at me with an intimidating stare. It was this same intimidation that the people lived under daily. They constantly lived in fear and distrust of everyone. It didn't matter if they had done anything wrong, all that was necessary was for there to be an allegation and they could end up in trouble. It was known by everyone that the hotels and, some believed, even the cars were bugged. They were always very careful not to be seen saying anything bad about Gaddafi or the regime, even if they felt that way. At times, some of the people I met would want desperately to share what their lives were really like. Naively I would ask questions out of curiosity. So, they would ask me to walk with them outside or in a corner away from everyone else and then they began to tell me about the abuses and oppressions that were commonplace in Libya.

Dealing with critics

Muammar Gaddafi's contradictory, ever-changing and idiosyncratic rule over Libya for more than forty years gave rise to unsatisfied citizens who formed opposition groups against his regime. He was able to stop several coups that endangered his government throughout the years but failed in 2011 as his opposition grew stronger and bigger and he gradually lost favor with his allies, forcing Gaddafi and his followers to commit bloodshed which angered Libyans even more and ended in his capture and brutal death at the hands of his critics.

Gaddafi's government had three types of opposition groups: the Islamists who wanted the return of Islamic traditions, the royalists who wanted the monarchy back in Libyan power and the democratic faction who wanted "true" democracy instead of the Libyan leader's somewhat tyrannical and dictatorial form of governance he called "democracy" (Blanchard & Zanotti, 2011). Even his very own military went against him at some point but were proven to be too weak to make a successful coup as Gaddafi once did to King Idris' monarchy in Libya. These enemies of the Gaddafi regime were handled with brute force by the Libyan leader's organized "people's courts" and "revolutionary committees," as well as by Libyan intelligence that monitored Libyan critics who were situated abroad (Black, 2000). They were blamed for harassment, intimidation, torture, murder and assassinations of alleged enemies that were a supposed threat to the regime. These opponents were often regarded as "stray dogs" (Blanchard & Zanotti, 2011, 19) who went against Gaddafi's belief that the formation of groups political in nature destroys the peace of the country and causes power struggles (Gaddafi, 1988). It was merely a matter of removing all threats to the Libyan government as much as possible. But due to the pressure of the United States and other nations that were trying to fix their relations with Libya, the government started making amends with several opposition individuals and groups and improving the country's human rights situation in the late 2000s (Blanchard & Zanotti, 2011). Despite these efforts, it was just too late for Gaddafi to mend what had already been said and done in the past. Libyans just grew tired and wanted changes after more than forty years under the Colonel's regime.

Gaddafi had focused on Islamdom and Arab unity since day one of becoming Libya's leader in 1969. Despite this, it was from his Muslim brothers that his opposition took root. He did implement and mold the country's new government based on Islamic beliefs, practices and teachings, but what angered Libya and the Arab world's Islamic clerics and fundamentalists was his "unorthodox[ed] approach to religion" (Greavette, 2005) as he imposed his own understanding and version of Islam. He tried making amends at first by banning alcohol and issuing other policies and restrictions based on traditional and conservative Islamic values, but then realized the holy men were of no use to him and to other Muslims when it comes to connecting with God. Gaddafi further challenged those individuals of the Islamic faith in 1978 when he replaced the Hadith, Islam's rulebook, with his self-authored *Green Book* to guide Libyans to the "right path" (Greavette, 2005). In relation to the *Green Book*, he allowed women to have equal rights and opportunities in Libya (Gaddafi, 1988), especially in providing them with free education and work, as well as allowing them to enter Libya's military. This led to the resignation in 1978 of the country's

Grand Mufti, Sheik Tahir al-Zawi, whom he never replaced with another (Greavette, 2005). Gaddafi's policies that were counter to Islamic values and restrictions led to the formation of several local Islamist groups within Libya such as the Muslim Brotherhood, the National Salvation Front, the Libyan Islamic Fighting Group (LIFG) and the Islamic Martyrdom Movement.

Despite Gaddafi's distrust of religious groups in Libya, as they tended to "become involved in politics, breeding factionalism, and undermining his revolutionary objectives" (Black, 2000, 257), as well as posing potential threats to his regime, he supported such groups outside Libya. He was very active in financially supporting terrorism in the 1980s. Aside from the strong opposition of these Islamist groups, Gaddafi's own officials disliked the Libyan leader's somewhat "bastardization" of the Islamic faith and his unwise decisions and activities in every aspect of Libyan society. Some of Libya's military personnel attempted coups several times but were too weak to overcome his armed forces and private security officers.

The Gaddafi government's 1972 Law Number 71 prohibited the creation of political parties and organizations (Blanchard & Zanotti, 2011). The religious group the Muslim Brotherhood originated from Libya's neighbor and former ally Egypt. In the 1940s, some of its members fled to Libya as their activities in Egypt were being heavily targeted by the government (Blanchard & Zanotti, 2011). They were regarded as a semi-recognized group in the country but were then imprisoned in 1973 when Gaddafi came to power. Despite this, the Muslim Brotherhood remained active but did most of its operations underground. They gradually attracted several Libyan civilians into their movement for change in Libya's government and Libyan society. Their message resonated especially with the urbanized and the poor, as the group's goal was to "reformulate Arab institutions along Islamic ideals" (Black, 2000, 258). With the Muslim Brotherhood's growing popularity, Gaddafi took heavy precautions, ordering the arrest of about 152 members in 1998. Two of the group's arrested leaders were given a death sentence and 70 of them were given a life imprisonment sentence during their trials in the early 2000s (Blanchard & Zanotti, 2011). Some of them died while in prison which caused rumors to circulate that they were being tortured under Gaddafi's orders. But by 2005, the Libyan government started to hold retrials and eventually released the remaining jailed Muslim Brotherhood members in 2006 (*BBC News*, 2011).

Historically, the Muslim Brotherhood is known for their advocacy for traditional Islamic teachings and for generally peaceful and nonviolent methods of protest as compared to its Libyan and Islam-based counterparts, the extremists (Black, 2000). This is what its main leader, Suleiman Abdel Qadir, has publicly emphasized: that the group only wished that Gaddafi give Libya sufficient political rights. Qadir's voice was eventually heard by the Libyan government in 2007 in the entity of Gaddafi's son Saif Al Islam, who was in charge of the country's human rights and political reforms, especially on the Libyan government having a more open and participative decision-making process in the different aspects of the state (Blanchard & Zanotti, 2011). Despite this, most of the Muslim Brotherhood's reform demands were never met, including the creation of a constitution for Libya and a set of civil rights for Libyans.

After the Muslim Brotherhood, the National Salvation Front was formed in 1981 in Libya. As compared to the former group, the NSF operated with force as it tried to gain members from Libya's armed forces (Black, 2000). Its main objective was to unite Gaddafi's enemies from both the secular and Islamist sectors in Libya in order to successfully overthrow the Libyan government and establish a new Libya.

By the 1990s, the capability and strength of opposition groups increased, as "anti-regime violence by Islamic extremists has reached new levels of intensity" (Black, 2000, 258). There had been an increase in the number of attempted assassinations of Colonel Gaddafi as new, better equipped and trained Libyan opposition groups emerged, as well as more brutal ones, such as the Islamic Martyrdom Movement and the notorious Libyan Islamic Fighting Group.

The Libyan Islamic Fighting Group or LIFG, which may have been one of the Gaddafi regime's most powerful enemies inside Libya, has also been involved in several terrorist attacks and has been engaged with other opposition groups and Islamic extremists in other countries. The group was known for coming close to successfully assassinating Gaddafi in 1996, for raiding Gaddafi's troops of their weaponry (Black, 2000), for allegedly participating in the May 2003 bombings in Casablanca in neighboring Morocco, and most especially, for being associated with Osama Bin Laden's Al Qaeda, the number one terrorist group on the U.S. list after the 9/11 attacks which killed thousands of Americans (Blanchard & Zanotti, 2011). Gaddafi and Western nations joined forces for the first time in the early 2000s in stopping the extremist group LIFG in its suspected operations that were inhumane and violent in nature like that of terrorism.

LIFG was secretly supported financially by several individuals and groups in the United States and in the United Kingdom. The U.S. government was able to reveal and freeze the group's assets in 2001, formally labeling it as a "foreign terrorist organization" in 2004, and was able to track down the group's financiers in the United Kingdom in 2006 and 2008 (Blanchard & Zanotti, 2011). These actions taken by the U.S. in fighting alleged terrorism in the form of the LIFG were marked with a suspected hidden agenda to further improve the country's relations with Gaddafi and Libya that would most likely benefit the United States in different angles. Despite these hindrances to the LIFG, the group's membership was plentiful, as it had some of its leaders and members situated in different parts of the globe recruiting more and more individuals for their cause, most especially in the United States and in several European countries.

In November 2007, the LIFG gained a higher level of terrorism and Islamic extremism as far as the Western powers were concerned. Two of Al Qaeda's prominent leaders, Abu Layth al Libi and Ayman al Zawahiri, revealed that the LIFG was affiliated with them (Blanchard & Zanotti, 2011). This announcement alarmed the United States and its allies as the extremist group LIFG was then viewed as an international threat instead of just being a danger to Gaddafi and his Libya. This was strongly denied by LIFG's leaders and members in the United Kingdom in a 2009 statement, wherein they emphasized that they differed "with others who use indiscriminate bombing and target civilians" (Blanchard & Zanotti, 2011). They argued that their opposition group was all about opposing the way Gaddafi was wrongly handling Libya and that they merely wanted the violence in their country to end through several political reforms.

Even before LIFG's recruitment of any affiliations with Al Qaeda in 2009, the Libyan government was involved in negotiations with LIFG's leaders to convince them to give up the group's reign of terror and violence, as well as their involvement with other extremist and terrorist groups. These talks were done under the Gaddafi Foundation with Saif Al Islam Gaddafi supervising the entire thing (Blanchard & Zanotti, 2011). Gaddafi's government and the LIFG eventually came to an agreement where the group would completely abandon its violent operations against the regime in exchange for the freedom of its arrested leaders and members, as well as the government addressing several of the group's demands for political, economic and social changes in Libya. This resulted in the release of about forty of its members and other Islamists from prison in 2009 immediately after the LIFG's leaders completed writing a series of recantations (Blanchard & Zanotti, 2011). Several years before, more than a hundred LIFG members were previously given their freedom.

Gaddafi did everything in his power to overpower and destroy his opposition and critics within Libya before they were able to pose a threat to his regime. Aside from a number of violent arrests of alleged opposition leaders and members in Libya, he launched intelligence personnel in other countries to investigate and monitor the activities of opposition groups that were suspected as being behind several assassinations and violent attacks against some of Libya's officials who were abroad. This led to the exile of several Libyan enemies of Gaddafi and the state. This included the leaders and members of the National Libyan Salvation Front (NLSF), the National Alliance, the Libyan Movement for Change and Reform, the Libyan National Movement, the Islamist Rally and the Republican Rally for Democracy and Justice, which also included a royalist movement under the former Libyan King Mohammed al Sanusi's grandson (Blanchard & Zanotti, 2011). While in exile, these Libyan opposition groups organized meetings, notably in the years 2005 and 2008, discussing plans on how to eradicate Gaddafi and his government from power over Libya and strategizing on putting up a new government once Libya was freed from the Gaddafi regime.

In relation to the Libyan state's efforts in negotiating with its enemies, government officials allowed exiled Libyans to come back home in exchange for agreeing to reconcile with the government by abandoning their operations and activities against Gaddafi's regime. In 2005 and 2006, about 800 exiles returned to the country and were followed by the return of 33 more in 2010 (Blanchard & Zanotti, 2011).

Despite efforts by Gaddafi and his government to fix its relationship with the Libyan opposition, some groups remained very active in their operations against the Libyan leader until Gaddafi himself resigned from power or committed to take steps towards economic, political and social reforms they wanted to happen in their country for a better Libya. This culminated in a brutal civil war in 2011 that eventually ended Gaddafi's reign of terror and his life.

Military plan

During the 1970s, Muammar Gaddafi began planning to purchase weapons of mass destruction (WMD) and eventually developing Libya's own WMD program to make Libya self-sufficient in defending itself. He also tried to improve Libya's very poor military during this time. This quickly alarmed the international community, especially the United States, out of concern Libya might use it for terrorism purposes. In 1976, Gaddafi stated that "atomic weapons will be like traditional ones, possessed by every state according to its potential. We will have our share of this new weapon" (Black, 2000, 247). He argued that Libya and other Arab nations should be allowed and able to have their own WMD in order to "defend themselves" from their enemies, especially the Western superpowers.

Despite this, Gaddafi kept Libya's WMD program hidden from the rest of the world for decades, publicly denying its existence to the United States and the United Kingdom who were investigating. They eventually found out the truth in 2003 when they caught Libya purchasing WMD components from Pakistan's "Father of the Nuclear Bomb," Dr. Abdul Qadeer Khan, and uranium centrifuges essential for WMD from Malaysia that were shipped via a German ship called BBC China bound for Libya which was seized by the United States (Donnelly & Serchuk, 2004). Gaddafi could have gotten away with it if he had abandoned developing Libya's own biological, chemical and nuclear weapons earlier as Libya's WMD programs were failing miserably.

Libya's military was composed of 50,000 personnel in the army, 40,000 in the Reserve People's Militia, 18,000 other armed forces, 8,000 in the navy, and 3,000 in the revolutionary guard corps during Gaddafi's last years as Libya's leader (Blanchard & Zanotti, 2011). It totaled to 119,000 military personnel in all, the biggest in the history of Libya, but was quite small for such a very large country. In addition to the shortage of personnel, Gaddafi's armed forces were armed with poorly maintained weaponry that largely outnumbered its military in terms of numbers (Blanchard & Zanotti). The country was understaffed and over-armed.

In line with Gaddafi's lack of trust and the incapability of the Libyan military, the Libyan leader focused more on financing weaponry rather than on improving his armed forces (Black, 2000). During the period of international sanctions against Libya, Gaddafi found it difficult to purchase arms from other countries as the Western nations feared that he would use them for terrorism since his regime had been blamed for several terrorist attacks in the 1980s. But when Libya's international relations improved, the arms embargo against the country was lifted by several nations beginning in 2004. In 2007, Gaddafi was allegedly able to purchase Milan anti-tank missiles from the European Aerospace and Defense Group (EADS). In 2008, he began negotiating with Russia on arms sales such as aircraft, air defense missiles, helicopters, and submarines, and by 2010, Libya allegedly purchased advanced air defense systems and Sukhoi Su-35 and Su-30 fighters (Blanchard & Zanotti, 2011). Despite these new weapons, which may have cost Libya a fortune, the Libyan leader failed to put them to use successfully in defending his regime in 2011.

Since Libya's military didn't pose a threat to any of its enemies, Gaddafi tried to develop the country's own WMD programs but with generally no success. He started in 1970 and continued to do so even during sanctions and embargos against Libya from the late 1980s to the early 2000s which caused a dramatic decline in the country's funds. Gaddafi never lost hope for decades before he finally revealed Libya's WMD in 2003, and gradually removed all traces of his WMD programs in the country. He formerly believed that "weapons can raise his international stature, deter the U.S. and Israeli attack[s], intimidate his neighbors, and serve as cheaper alternatives to more expensive conventional forces" (Black, 2000, 259). Gaddafi spent billions of dollars of Libya's funds in creating nuclear, biological and chemical weapons

81

but mainly faced several hindrances in doing so because of the lack of equipment, suppliers and foreign assistance, as well as poor management.

Gaddafi's main focus in terms of WMD was the creation of nuclear weapons for Libya. The country's membership to the Nuclear Non-Proliferation Treaty (NPT) did not stop him from his goal he had so long been obsessed with. Since Libya lacked the knowledge or resources to make nuclear weaponry, he attempted to secretly purchase the technology he needed from Argentina, France, Japan, Pakistan and the Soviet Union in the 1970s but with no success (Blanchard & Zanotti, 2011). He also failed in acquiring a nuclear bomb from China in 1970 and from Russia in 1992. Gaddafi came very close when he sponsored Pakistan's nuclear weapons program in the 1970s in order to acquire a so-called "Islamic Bomb" (Black, 2000, 260) that was being developed, up until Pakistan's Prime Minister and ally Ali Bhutto's execution in 1979 shattered any possibility. But in 1997, Gaddafi's hopes for Pakistan's nuclear weapons technology rekindled. His government was able to reach an agreement with Dr. Abdul Qadeer Khan, Pakistan's then leading nuclear scientist, to provide a weapons design and uranium-based technology Libya needed (Blanchard & Zanotti, 2011). Gaddafi secretly purchased the materials needed for the project from different factories and suppliers around the world up until 2003 when the United States was able to catch him in the act upon the seizure of the BBC China which contained nuclear technology equipment headed for Libya (Donnelly & Serchuk, 2004). This marked the end of Libya's WMD programs.

The only actual achievement Gaddafi attained in his nuclear weapons obsession was in 1979 with the creation of a nuclear research center in Tajura. It had a small research reactor which was purchased from the Soviet Union (Black, 2000).

Like Gaddafi's quest for nuclear weapons despite Libya's membership to a treaty that rejects such weapons, he pursued biological weapons despite being one of the signatories of the Biological Weapons Convention (Black, 2000). But like Libya's nuclear weapons program, it failed to achieve anything due to the lack of equipment, knowledge, technology, and trained personnel.

Of all the billions of dollars spent on Libya's attempts to develop its own WMD, its chemical warfare program was by far most successful but was not of much use to Gaddafi. In the 1980s, the government was able to establish production plants in Sebha, Rabta and Tarhuna, which all had adequate equipment and technology purchased from several companies in Asia and Europe (Blanchard & Zanotti, 2011). These plants were able to make about a hundred tons of chemical weapons which included mustard and nerve gases (Black, 2000). But due to the international fuss that Libya's successful chemical weapons production made in the late 1980s, the government was forced to shut down its factory in Rabta to avoid any further controversy following Gaddafi's bad relations with the United States and other nations. It was eventually reopened in 1996 (Black, 2000).

Libya's WMD program was generally a failure and a waste of billions of dollars the country acquired from oil revenues that was supposed to be allocated in more feasible government projects that could have benefited the Libyan people. But what if Gaddafi actually had succeeded in attaining his desire for WMD?

The reason behind Gaddafi's thirst for Libya's own WMD was centered on going against the United States and other nations including Israel instead of "defending" Libya as the Libyan leader continuously claimed. The United States was actually able to identify five strategies that Gaddafi was most likely going for.

The first strategy behind Libya's WMD programs was to make the United States appear as a "bully," ganging up on Libya once it decided to intervene in the country's affairs, especially its WMD (Black, 2000). This could have been possible, as Gaddafi would threaten his North African neighbors, some European countries and even Israel with using his WMD on them if they joined forces with the U.S. in destroying his regime.

The second possible strategy if Libya's WMD programs did push through was to utilize WMD in attacking the United States' military bases found in different locations in other countries (Black, 2000). These attacks could have triggered the withdrawal of U.S. armed forces from foreign bases, especially in the African continent and the Arab world, due to the increasing fear of more killings of the Western country's servicemen.

In contrast to the withdrawal outcome, the third strategy would take care of the possibility that the U.S. would end up seeking revenge for the death of its soldiers. Libya would make use of its

WMD in defeating the United States' attack force, hopefully causing thousands and thousands of deaths on the United States' side (Black, 2000). This would then end in a peace negotiation between the two conflicting countries instead of the Western superpower sending out more troops for retaliation against Libya.

If the United States and its allies actually had won in battle, the fourth strategy involved Gaddafi staying in power despite Libya's defeat as his winning enemies would choose to negotiate rather than risk more casualties from both sides (Black, 2000).

The worst-case scenario for Gaddafi, which scared him from the start, was the destruction of his regime due to foreign intervention. Just in case this happened, the fifth WMD strategy made sure that the Libyan leader would be able to successfully take revenge on his enemies. This horrendous possibility would be inevitable since "with nothing left for Gaddafi to lose, there would be little that could be done to deter him" (Black, 2000, 261).

Fortunately, these scenarios will forever remain as what-ifs instead of realities since the Colonel decided to diminish all his plans for WMD domination in exchange for better foreign relations, and especially now that he is dead. Had he developed the weapons, he could have defeated his enemies before they could defeat him, but in the end, he wasn't able to.

Leadership Lessons

Creativity is an important trait of leaders. To some, Gaddafi's very whimsical persona might be construed as creative. Yet, the country never really became known for anything great. Libya was never involved in any great scientific, educational or other advances. Instead, all of these areas suffered under Gaddafi. Whenever people had a choice, they would go to other countries for medical care and get private education, because the system was so lacking. This did not need to be the case, because unlike other countries in Africa, Libya had great oil wealth and could have been very prosperous.

When I think of great leaders, I think of risk takers. The only area that Gaddafi exhibited the leadership attribute of being a risk taker was in his sponsorship and involvement of terrorism. He actively pursued sponsoring and supporting groups that he saw as revolutionaries or freedom fighters.

Hand in hand with being a risk taker, is courage. Gaddafi was described as a coward by many who worked with him. He was always paranoid about his country being invaded, which was why he took all the English language off the street signs. In addition, he did not like to fly and was fearful of something happening to him when he was traveling, so he had his staff develop elaborate escape routes.

Chapter 7: Gaddafi's foreign relations

Gaddafi's relationships with other political leaders had been rough all throughout his reign in Libya. He made friends, but he made more enemies and these friendships were generally short-lived. According to Harvey Kushner (2003), Gaddafi's "experiences shaped his extreme view of international relation[s]. His beliefs and statements have often appeared inexplicable to outside observers; many have characterized him as eccentric, and some have gone so far to call him mad" (303). In the end, despite regaining a good working relationship with most of his former enemies by the 2000s, Gaddafi lost the trust and respect of the international community due to the actions he made against his own people who were growing unhappy and angry with his contradictory and idiosyncratic way of governing Libya and its citizens.

Quest for Arab unity

Upon his proclamation of himself as Libya's leader, Gaddafi focused on achieving Arab unity, in relation to his political model and all-time idol, former Egyptian president Abdel Nasser. He wanted Libya and other Arab nations to become the world's superpowers, overpowering the Western world (Black, 2000). But due to his revolutionary idealism and ever-changing attitude towards politics, Gaddafi instead was ignored by most conservative Arab countries, which greatly pained his regime all throughout as Libya suffered isolation from the Arab world.

In 1969, Gaddafi established the short-lived Federation of Arab Republics (FAR) immediately after successfully overthrowing the Libyan monarchy. The FAR's first objective was to politically unite neighboring Arab nations Egypt, Sudan and Libya. It was supposed to be led by Egypt's Nasser as president, and Libya's Gaddafi and Sudan's Numeiry. Numiery was then replaced by Syria's Hafez al-Assad when Numeiry suddenly backed out from the union as vice-president (Greavette, 2005). But before Gaddafi's pan-Arab movement was able to take shape and push through, Nasser unexpectedly passed away and was immediately replaced by Anwar Sadat who proved to be an enemy rather than an ally to the Libyan leader. In 1973, Libya and Egypt got into a conflict when Sadat rejected Gaddafi's orders to sink the Queen Elizabeth II ocean liner that was on its way to Israel with a number of traveling American and European Jews after Israel mistakenly sunk a Libyan airliner along the Sinai Peninsula (Greavette, 2005). This incident led to the fall-out of the FAR and Egypt deciding to cut its political relations with Libya due to Gaddafi being a threat to Egypt's security. Gaddafi never lost faith in forming political unions with other nations, especially with other Arab countries, as he reached out to Algeria, Burkina Faso, Chad, Malta, Mauritania, Morocco, Sudan, Syria, Tunisia and even the People's Republic of China (Greavette, 2005). None of these attempts ever moved forward as the Libyan leader's terms were very demanding and too idealistic for the taste of these countries' respective leaders and governments.

Aside from Arab unity, Gaddafi was obsessed with bringing Israel down, a goal which he shared with most Arab nations. He was very devastated after the disastrous and embarrassing results of the 1967 and 1974 Arab wars against Israel and came to the conclusion that Israel could only be dealt with by propaganda, terrorism and diplomacy (Greavette, 2005). He remained very angry about Israel's existence as he wanted the territory to be given back to the Palestinian people. He remained unmoved to any "negotiation or reconciliation with Israel throughout the Cold War era and the 1990s, promoting armed struggle as the only viable means to end Israel's occupation of territory it captured from neighboring Arab states in 1967" (Blanchard & Zanotti, 2011, 6). This was contradictory to the view of Egypt's Sadat, as well as that of the Palestine Liberation Organization (PLO) leader Yasir Arafat, which caused years of conflict. Gaddafi eventually reconciled with Arafat in 1987 and provided the PLO and other Palestinian groups with financial support and training. He welcomed them to Libya with open arms until the second half of the 1990s (Blanchard & Zanotti, 2011). He continued to object to any kind of peace process and continuously tried to urge other political leaders of the Arab world to reject any type of negotiation with Israel, in hopes of isolating Israel. Due to Gaddafi's controversial viewpoint on the Israel-Palestine conflict, he was ignored by Jordan, Saudi Arabia and the Gulf states (Black, 2000). He also made enemies with Iraq's notorious dictator Saddam Hussein due to Gaddafi's support for Iran at the time of the Iran-Iraq War. He also strongly rejected the Arab League's Arab Peace Initiative, which he felt was not advantageous for the Palestinian people, who remained without a state or territory of their own, and did not necessarily represent the stand of all Arab nations including Libya (Blanchard & Zanotti, 2011).

But in recent years, in line with Libya's efforts to rebuild its international relations, Gaddafi's view on Israel dramatically mellowed as he instead urged for both the Israelis and the Palestinians to live peacefully in one, single state he called "Isratine." He strongly advocated for this idea of his rather than supporting a two-state solution which other members of the Arab world and the international community have been suggesting for years to end the conflict (Greavette, 2005). Aside from this, he wanted Israel to allow the return of homes and properties of Palestinian refugees before 1948 (Blanchard & Zanotti, 2011). All of Gaddafi's suggestions were rejected by Israel and its allies.

Aside from promoting political unification within the Arab world, Gaddafi also made it a point to establish good relations with Libya's neighboring North African nations. But the result of his efforts was the exact opposite as he was in a continuous conflict with five of Libya's neighbors. In Algeria and Tunisia, the Libyan leader threatened their respective governments by supporting their opposition groups as the two African countries didn't have Libya's back when it was given international sanctions by the United Nations (Black, 2000). Egyptian and Libyan relations fell out when Nasser died and Sadat took over the presidency. In 1977, Egypt attacked Libya after the supposed assassination plot of Gaddafi against Sadat, as informed by an Israeli intelligence (Black, 2000). As for Chad, the conflict was a matter of territory and economic gain. In 1974 the Libyan government claimed that Chad's Auzo strip was

Libya's, which had rich uranium deposits essential for its economy, as well as its then WMD programs (Black, 2000). That led Gaddafi's forces into an unsuccessful occupation of the region and a shameful defeat by Chad's armed troops. It was only Niger that didn't pose a threat to Libya and was eventually one of the Gaddafi regime's weak allies that was of no use to him.

Gaddafi also tried developing political friendship with sub-Saharan African nations. His agenda was to spread Libyan influence over Western and Israeli influence in Africa. The Libyan leader tried winning over several political figures in the continent, especially the notorious and dictatorial ones, such as the Central African Republic's Bokassa, Liberia's Taylor, Sierra Leone's Sankoh, the Democratic Republic of Congo's Kabila, Chad's Deby, Burkina Faso's Compaore, Uganda's Amin and Zaire's Mobuto. He provided all with arms and training in Libya's own military training camps (Black, 2000). In Liberia, Gaddafi provided then President Charles Taylor with weaponry such as ammunition, grenades, missiles and mortars, to fight off the United States and the rest of the international community trying to remove Taylor from office (Donnelly & Serchuk, 2004). In Zimbabwe, he backed up President Robert Mugabe in 2001 when his brutal rule was falling apart. Gaddafi gave a million dollars for the country's re-elections favoring Mugabe and promised to give Zimbabwe $360 million of oil every year (Donnelly & Serchuk, 2004). This support for such African leaders led to the denial of Gaddafi's chairmanship of the Organization of African Unity (OAU).

Shift to Africa

When Libya was given a series of international sanctions and embargos by the United Nations and most of the international organization's member states, the country received very little support from the Arab world. Gaddafi grew frustrated and angry and eventually decided to shift his attention from pan-Arabism to pan-Africanism in the 1990s (Blanchard & Zanotti, 2011). Gaddafi supported South Africa's Nelson Mandela and helped in the peace negotiations in Congo, Eritrea, Liberia, Sierra Leone and Sudan in the 1990s. These efforts eventually paid off in 1998 when other African leaders who were members of the OAU agreed to ignore the airline embargo imposed by the UN against Libya. Gaddafi then reciprocated by giving these leaders and their respective countries large sums of money for every violation they committed against the embargo (Black, 2000). Aside from this, the Libyan leader pushed for a "United States of Africa" (Blanchard & Zanotti, 2011, 25). This notion was eventually rejected by most of his African allies as there seemed to be a hidden agenda which involved Gaddafi being made the leader of the suggested single African state. But there was no denying that the Libyan leader had power over the continent with all the support he had provided for most of Africa (Donnelly & Serchuk, 2004). This deeply concerned the United States and its allies in the 1990s until the early 2000s when Libya began negotiations with the U.S. for the sake of good international relations as Libya was continuously suffering the consequences of international sanctions and embargos which began in the 1980s.

By 2009, Gaddafi was made the chairman of the African Union. Upon his chairmanship, he pushed for African unity, as well as urging "for a more powerful voice for the African Union in international bodies" (Blanchard & Zanotti, 2011, 25) in hopes to gain more international opportunities for the continent. He tried to renew his position in order to continue his advocacy in 2010 but failed to do so due to lack of support from other members of the organization.

Cold War tensions

In 1969, during the successful coup of Gaddafi and his men, the Soviet Union was having naval exercises on the Cyrenaica coast in Libya. Upon hearing the news about Gaddafi being proclaimed as Libya's new leader, the then communist superpower in the East "considered [Libya] as being a good recruitment prospect" (Greavette, 2005). After a fall-out with Egypt under Sadat in the 1970s, the Soviets saw Libya as a prospective military ally to substitute for Egypt in the Mediterranean region. They were hoping that Gaddafi's regime would grant them access to Libya's airfields and ports, as well that they would get their hands on the country's billions of dollars in oil treasure in exchange for the arms they would be providing the regime with (Greavette, 2005). In 1971, in order to somehow win Gaddafi over, the Soviet Union gave the Libyan leader one of the most prestigious awards of the state, the Order of Lenin. The awarding was held in Moscow and was supposedly based on the Libyan leader's contribution in ensuring "peace in the world" (Simons, 1996). But this growing relationship proved to be short-lived. In 1972, Gaddafi grew angry with the Soviets' alleged assistance of India against Pakistan, a Muslim nation, followed by the Soviets' lack of support for Egypt in terms of supplying Libya's neighbor with weaponry.

Gaddafi eventually regretted his cooperation with the Soviet Union as the United States grew threatened by the Libya-Soviet Union "partnership" at the height of the Cold War. The Libyan leader's mentor and role model Nasser warned him in his first years about engaging with the Soviet Union and angering or going against the United States in any way. Despite this, Gaddafi argued earlier in his reign that it was "necessary to take up the Soviets' offer of arms and economic cooperation to help compensate for the Egyptian tilt towards the Americans" (Greavette, 2005). And in 1970, he purchased arms from the Soviet Union, as well as Chieftain tanks from the United Kingdom and a hundred Mirage fighter planes from France (Simon, 1996). The rest of the 1970s proved to be of mutual benefit between Libya and the Soviet Union. But as Gaddafi's relationship with the United States and its allies was falling apart in the 1980s, the Soviets declined to give any support to Libya since the Colonel proved to be unpredictable on his viewpoints and took actions that had been proven to be dangerous. At the same time Libya rejected the Soviets' request to put military bases in the country.

Upon Gaddafi's takeover of Libya, the United States and other Western superpowers did not view the Libyan leader's regime as a threat. This was despite Gaddafi's controversial views on international politics. They instead chose to ignore the Libyan leader despite Libya "drifting away from the Western sphere of influence [since] the Americans did not view Gaddafi as [a] key player on either the Middle East or the World stage" (Greavette, 2005). This was despite his support for international opposition groups that were viewed as terrorists in the 1970s and the 1980s, his partnership with the Soviets during the Cold War and his advocacies against Israel.

Ignorance eventually turned into utmost attention and concern from the international community in the early 1980s when Ronald Reagan became the U.S. president. Reagan was a soldier during the onset of the Cold War where he grew his dislike for Nasser's idealism, which Gaddafi idolized and utilized in shaping Libya under his regime. This influenced the U.S. president in his actions towards Libya, as well as his belief that "radical leaders such as Gaddafi had lost respect for American power and prowess in the post-Vietnam era" (Greavette, 2005), which he planned on correcting. Reagan also earlier viewed the growing conflicts in different parts of the world, especially in the Arab world, as one of the Soviet Union's strategies for overpowering the Western superpowers (Simons, 1996). This was eventually met with mixed reactions from other countries, some supporting Reagan's view while others regarded the U.S. president's campaign against Libya as preposterous. Some European nations argued that the U.S. should focus more on Syria and Iran who were obviously a threat to international security as they encouraged terrorism on a deeper, more dangerous level than Libya under Gaddafi. With President Reagan's campaign launch against the Gaddafi regime in 1981, Europe grew fearful of the possibility of Libya strengthening its relations with the Soviet Union as the consequence of the United States' actions. Some of these European nations even blamed the Reagan administration for the actions taken by Gaddafi in the 1980s such as his sponsorship of terrorism and alleged Libyan attacks on American and European military personnel and civilians. They regarded the campaign as misleading since the U.S. established "Gaddafi as a lunatic; Libya as a Soviet proxy; Gaddafi as the major source of international terrorism; and the

Libyan regime as being extremely repressive in nature" (Greavette, 2005) to the rest of the international community.

Reagan pushed his campaign against Gaddafi and Libya in the early 1980s even further when he sought trading embargos to decrease the country's oil revenues and completely isolate Libya from the rest of the world diplomatically and politically. In addition the U.S. president called Gaddafi several distasteful names and adjectives like the "mad dog of the Middle East" (Donnelly & Serchuk, 2004) and being "crazy like a fox" (Greavette, 2005). Then the U.S. Secretary of State Alexander Haig even called the Libyan leader a "cancer that had to be removed" (Greavette, 2005), which was then followed by then Vice President George Bush's remark that the Colonel was an "egomaniac who would trigger World War III to make headlines" (Greavette, 2005). These resulted in the lifetime hatred of Gaddafi and Reagan for each other. For Gaddafi and his then allies amidst the growing U.S.-Libyan conflict, the United States was a "bully," dominating every country that it viewed as weak. They often called the Western superpower "the Devil" and "Satan" (Greavette, 2005) as they claimed that the U.S. was the source of all the evils in the world such as capitalism and imperialism. Gaddafi also went on to criticize and ridicule Americans on why they chose a Hollywood actor who had no clue of what was happening in the world outside the movies as their president and the most powerful man in the world (Greavette, 2005). Reagan and Gaddafi's hatred for each other deepened from a political to a personal manner, as they publicly attacked each other's private life whenever they had the chance.

The worsening U.S.-Libya power struggle was highlighted by several continuous incidents of attacks from both sides in the 1980s. In 1983, the United States suspected that Gaddafi was plotting and sending out assassination personnel to take out American ambassadors and officials in Egypt, France, Italy and Spain, as well as in Washington in order to allegedly assassinate President Reagan (Greavette, 2005). The Libyan leader denied such claims, but allowed a series of attacks on the American embassy in Libya's capital, Tripoli, and had Libya's embassies, then called Libyan People's

Bureaus abroad, provide Gaddafi's allies with arms. These actions resulted in bloodshed for the first time in 1984 when a British policewoman named Yvonne Fletcher was killed in London as anti-Gaddafi protesters stormed the Libyan embassy in the city. This also led to the arrest of six British individuals who were in Libya as hostages in exchange for the avoidance of the condemnation of the Libyan embassy officials for the death of the policewoman (Greavette, 2005). Previously in 1981, American and Libyan armed forces came into a clash as two of Libya's fighter jets tried to exercise territorial power over the nearby Gulf of Sidra when they viewed two American fighter jets in its skies. This eventually ended with the shooting down of Libya's jets. The incident eventually led to Gaddafi forming a military pact with Ethiopia and Yemen against the so-called "David Alliance" that was composed of the United States, Egypt, Sudan and Israel.

In 1985, a series of bombings occurred in different locations that involved several deaths of U.S. servicemen which were eventually blamed on Libya by the United States (Simons, 1996). The first of these attacks was the bombing of Northwest Orient Airlines' office in Copenhagen, followed by the bombing of a café near a U.S. embassy in the city of Rome (Blanchard & Zanotti, 2011). In the same year, a hijacking transpired in Egyptian waters of the Achille Lauro, an Italian ship, which caused the death of several American hostages (Greavette, 2005). The hijackers were then welcomed and given a celebration in Libya's capital Tripoli by Gaddafi. This greatly angered not only the United States, but also the United Nations. The Libyan leader was a no-show in the international organization's fortieth anniversary celebration in New York after the incident. The alleged attacks by Gaddafi continued in late 1985 when a group of Libyan armed forces under the command of Abu Nidal operating outside the country apprehended an Egypt Air jet plane and made a series of attacks on Israeli El Al located in airports in Rome and Vienna (Greavette, 2005). These terrorist attacks by Libyan military personnel resulted in 25 casualties, which included five Americans.

By the following year, the ongoing Libya-U.S. conflict was at its peak as more and more violent attacks led to more casualties and damages, totally causing chaos in the international community. The State of Libya started claiming a 200-mile economic zone and a larger territory by the Mediterranean Sea along the Gulf of Sidra which the U.S. then regarded as a challenge to the Western country's right for a free pass and access in the Libyan-claimed waters (Simons, 1996). This resulted in the U.S. Operation Prairie Fire, a military exercise where the U.S. military's Sixth Fleet entered the Gulf of Sidra which Libya proclaimed as theirs (Greavette, 2005). This led to a series of missile exchanges that took down several of Libya's fighter jets and boats without doing any harm to the United States' fleet. This last clash between the two countries wounded Gaddafi and his regime pretty badly as Libya was not supported by the allies the Libyan leader thought his country had. This included the Soviet Union's denial of having anything to do with Gaddafi, as Anatoliy Dobyrin, the Soviet Union's Ambassador to the United States, stated that "Libya was an American problem" (Greavette, 2005) and not his country's problem.

The series of events that weren't generally in favor of Libya deeply angered and frustrated Colonel Gaddafi, forcing him to take far more drastic actions against the United States and its allies that were viewed as terrorist in nature by most outsiders. This led to the series of bombings and attacks on planes abroad in 1986 which Gaddafi mostly denied having anything to do with, namely the TWA Flight 840 explosion and the LaBelle nightclub bombing which resulted in the deaths of several Americans (Blanchard & Zanotti, 2011). This hit the United States in its core and forced the Reagan administration to take drastic and violent actions against Gaddafi and Libya.

In 1986 following the TWA Flight 840 explosion and the LaBelle nightclub bombing, the United States launched Operation Eldorado Canyon that consisted of a series of 24 plane attacks on the Gaddafi regime's government and military centers located in Benghazi and Tripoli (Greavette, 2005). This attack resulted in about thirty Libyan casualties. The United States' bloody revenge against Libya also resulted in forever scarring Gaddafi and his family. One of the bombing's targets was the private residence of the Libyan leader located in the large Bab el-Azziziya Barrack, in hopes that it would successfully kill the Libyan leader (Simons, 1996). It instead resulted in the alleged death of Gaddafi's sixteen-month-old adopted daughter named Hana due to brain damage as the result of the explosion (*Hindustan Times*, 2011) and the injuries of his wife and his three children. Later that day of the series of U.S. bombings in Libya, the Colonel launched missiles targeted to Lampedusa, an island in nearby Italy that was home to a U.S. navigation center, but failed to do any damage as the missiles embarrassingly fell short (Greavette, 2005).

Following these exchanges of attacks in 1986, both Libya under Gaddafi's regime and the United States under the Reagan administration gained the sympathy, as well as the ridicule of different members of the international community. With the brutal bombing of Libya by the U.S., Gaddafi was received with compassion as America's attack became too personal with the death of the Libyan leader's daughter and the injuries his family suffered (Simons, 1996). In Libya, Gaddafi's critics diverted their hatred to the United States as they considered the Western superpower's actions as inhumane and below the belt. In the United States' defense, it was high time for Libya to have a taste of its own medicine, and the attacks were meant to discourage any other political leaders and nations from pursuing any terrorist attacks against other countries (Greavette, 2005). Gaddafi grew more and more frustrated with the result of his duel with the United States, which was considered as a turning point for the Libyan leader in terms of his ideology and political beliefs. The United States' obvious superiority over Libya put the Gaddafi regime's operations into low key. This was until another series of bombings from 1988 to 1989 that targeted American servicemen and civilians, which was immediately blamed on the Libyan leader by the United States, the United Nations and the rest of the international community because of Gaddafi's support for terrorism around the globe.

Gaddafi's sponsorship of terrorism

In line with Muammar Gaddafi's quest for world domination through the destruction of capitalism, imperialism and the Western sphere of influence, he was very active in sponsoring several terrorist groups and nations around the globe that he felt had the same point of view as his. The Libyan leader's alleged support of "some 50 terror organizations and subversion groups, and to more than 40 radical governments in Africa, Asia, Europe, and America" (Black, 2000, 256) angered not only the Western superpowers, but also the Arab world. Instead of gaining more allies, it resulted in Libya suffering from international isolation for more than a decade due to a series of international sanctions and embargos given to the country in the following years.

Gaddafi offered support by different means such as financial assistance, arms supplies and military training from the time he became Libya's leader until his death in 2011 (Greavette, 2005). The terrorist groups he supported were known for their acts of violence as it was the only way of making their supposed good intentions possible. Some of these notorious U.S.-identified terrorists within the African continent and the Arab world were the Palestinian Abu Nidal Organization, which Gaddafi remained very supportive of until his last years in power (Black, 2000); West Africa's Revolutionary United Front (RUF), which was known for the bloody hacking of individuals in Sierra Leone under Foday Sankoh's commands (Donnelly & Serchuk, 2004); the Popular Front for the Liberation of Palestine (PFLP) under George Habash, and the National Patriotic Front of Liberia under Charles Taylor. In Europe and Asia, Libya's state-sponsored terrorism expanded to the Irish Republican Army (IRA) and the Red Army Faction, even reaching extremist groups in the Philippine archipelago.

Since 1969, Gaddafi built and established several training camps around Libya to cater to the "freedom fighters" from different parts of the world he was supporting. His first beneficiaries were several Palestinian factions under his long-time friend Abu Nidal, as well as Abu Musa (Greavette, 2000). The Colonel expanded the reach of his military training by the 1980s in Sinawin, Tubrug and Zuwarah. These additional Libyan training camps offered one of the best military trainings during that time as different experts from Libya, Palestine, Cuba, Russia, North Korea, Iran, Syria, Bulgaria and the Czech Republic, as well as from Britain and United States, which included former and retired CIA personnel, were hired by Gaddafi to instruct the camps' trainees (Greavette, 2000). Despite these efforts, the Libyan leader failed to get anything in return from most of the terrorist groups he helped in almost all means to succeed in their respective objectives for their operations and activities.

By the second half of the 1980s, Gaddafi became one of the United States' prominent international enemies with the series of bombings in different locations during this time that were immediately blamed on the Libyan leader as they evidently targeted the Western superpower. He was the prime suspect due to his continuous sponsorship for terrorism prior to the bombings.

In 1986, a bombing of the LaBelle nighttclub in Germany's capital, Berlin, claimed the lives of two U.S. servicemen (Donnelly & Serchuk, 2004). They were Sgt. Kenneth T. Ford and Sgt. James E. Goins (Blanchard & Zanotti, 2011). About 80 other U.S. military men and women were injured during the bombing.

The 1986 United States' bombing of Libya, code-named Operation El Dorado Canyon, comprised air strikes by the United States against Libya on April 15, 1986. The attack was carried out by the U.S. Air Force, Navy and Marine Corps via air strikes, in response to the 1986 Berlin discotheque bombing. The attack began at 0200 hours (Libyan time), and lasted about twelve minutes, with military targets. Some bombs landed off-target, striking diplomatic and civilian sites in Tripoli and Benghazi.

Pan Am 103

On December 21, 1988, came the bombing of bombing of Pan Am Flight 103 over Lockerbie in Scotland. The plane came from London and was headed to New York (Blanchard & Zanotti, 2011). This claimed the lives of 259 passengers and crew members on board with no survivors, including 11 victims that were on the ground (Greavette, 2005). This deeply enrage the United States, Scotland and the United Nations. They meticulously investigated the tragic incident that they suspected was a terrorist attack and did everything possible to find out who was behind the attack. After a long investigation, they were able to identify two suspects in 1991, namely Libyan intelligence agents Abdel Basset Al Megrahi, who was then Tripoli's Center for Strategic Studies head, and Al Amin Khalifah Fhimah, who was the director of Libya's airlines office located in Malta (Greavette, 2005). In 1999, after the Gaddafi government handed over the two primary suspects, a series of trials were held under a Scottish court at a former NATO air base called Camp Van Zeist. Megrahi was found to be guilty and was convicted with a life sentence which he was to serve in a Scottish prison, while Fhimah was found not guilty and was acquitted of any crime surrounding the Lockerbie bombing.

The last of the series of bombings was in 1989 with the bombing of the French airline UTA Flight 772 over Western Africa's Niger. This claimed the lives of 171 passengers and crew members on board, which included seven Americans (Donnelly & Serchuk, 2004). By 1999, six Libyans were found guilty of the bombing by a French court (Blanchard & Zanotti, 2011).

Despite the involvement of Libyan individuals in the three bombings, Gaddafi strongly denied his government's participation in the actions of the proven guilty Libyans despite their highly probable connection with the Libyan leader. He denied that they were under any command by him. Despite the lack of sufficient evidence to pin him down, the United States and its allies, as well as the United Nations, proclaimed international sanctions and embargos against Libya until Gaddafi and his government admitted to the series of bombings. This proclamation left the Libyan leader with no friends and allies and the Libyans with economic struggles and high poverty.

Leadership Lessons

Determination is a very important attribute of leadership. Gaddafi was definitely determined to be a leader of a great nation, at whatever cost. Initially he set his sights on Arab unity. When he was rejected by the Arab nations, he turned his focus on becoming the King of Africa. He attempted to unify the African leaders in creating the United States of Africa, with himself as the self-appointed leader. The challenge is that in a true collaboration, there must be respect and honor for the other parties, and he lacked that. In fact, on many occasions he spoke ill of the "black leaders," seeing them as subservient to himself. So, he decided to try to buy their support, by giving significant financial contributions to the African leaders. That got him elected briefly as the head of the African Union, where he promptly declared himself the "King of Kings" of Africa. This just further drew contempt for him by the other African leaders.

Chapter 8: Revival of foreign relations - Gaddafi's change of heart

The United Nations ordered sanctions against Libya from 1992 to 1999. These sanctions were ordered because of the acts of state-sponsored terrorism Colonel Muammar Gaddafi was found connected to. These sanctions "crippled the Libyan economy and isolated the country from the world community" (Black, 2000, 256) for a long period of time. These sanctions were designed to put pressure on Gaddafi to stop his sponsorship of terrorism.

The UN made its sanctions effective on April 15, 1992, when Libya failed to appear at trial under the International Criminal Court (ICC) for the crimes it had committed in the 1980s (Greavette, 2005). The sanctions included a travel ban and international embargos to put the country's oil, its main source of revenue, in deep trouble. By the first half of the 1990s, Libya's oil revenue fell from $25 billion in the 1980s to an ultimate low of merely $7 billion, yet Libya still remained as one of Africa's leading economies as compared to its highly poor neighbors (Greavette, 2005). As for Gaddafi's state-sponsored terrorism, he continued that activity into the 1990s but in a lesser degree and on a low-profile basis.

The Libyan leader grew disenchanted by the lack of support from other countries, especially from Libya's neighbors, whom he thought were his friends or allies (Black, 2000). His assistance of other political leaders and international groups proved to be more detrimental than helpful to his regime, as he instead made more enemies in the international community. Despite the pressure he was under, Gaddafi remained insistent that his government wasn't involved in any of the allegations made against him, arguing that the actions of the Libyans involved in a series of terrorist attacks were by no means connected to him or any of Libya's policies under his regime.

The effects of "a loss of oil revenue, restrictions on the travel of senior officials, an international travel ban, and an arms embargo against Libya eventually took its toll on Gaddafi's government and Libya's citizens and economy" (Blanchard & Zanotti, 2011, 7). With Gaddafi losing hope of ever overpowering the United States and its allies with the use of his controversial ideologies and perception of international politics, as well as the manipulation of his then "imaginary allies," the Libyan leader started to change his ways in 1999. This was in hopes of regaining good relations with foreign countries, especially with the United States, and re-establishing Libya in the international community after its isolation from the rest of the world for so long.

The most probable reasons behind Gaddafi's sudden change of heart were his disillusionment with the Arab world he formerly wanted to unite to rule over the Western superpowers, and his disillusionment with his revolutionary movement which he admittedly stated was very weak (Greavette, 2005). The Libyan leader was very frustrated with the other Arab nations' lack of back-up for his regime during Libya's "darkest hours." He went on to state that it would be better to cooperate with the United States and Israel instead of working with the Arab world after everything that had happened (Greavette, 2005). This eventually led to Gaddafi's shift to pan-Africanism beginning in the early 2000s (Blanchard & Zanotti, 2011). As for his earlier ideologies that generally rested in fanaticism, the Colonel eventually replaced them with that of pragmatism (Greavette, 2005), out of desperation and the necessity for Libya to have better international relations.

In 1999, after many years of suffering under international sanctions and embargos, Libya agreed to hand over the two Libyan intelligence agents, Megrahi and Fhimah, who were the primary suspects behind the 1988 Lockerbie bombing, to stand trial (Blanchard & Zanotti, 2011). The trial took place at a special court set up at a former NATO air base called Camp Van Zeist in the Netherlands. It was convened under Scottish law, with Scottish attorneys and Scottish high court judges presiding over the case. The trial lasted for 84 days and the court found Megrahi guilty and Fhimah not guilty (Greavette, 2005). In addition to this, several years later Libya also agreed to compensate the UTA Flight 772 victims and their families. This eventually led to the removal of most of the international sanctions and embargos against Libya, especially by the United Nations, the United Kingdom and several other European countries in 1999 (Donnelly & Serchuk, 2004). Despite these positive steps Gaddafi took in mending his relations with the international community, the United States remained unmoved. It maintained its embargo against Libya under the 1996 Iran-Libya Sanctions Act (ILSA).

The "changed" Gaddafi continued to pursue the United States to further prove that Libya was ready to get involved and to actively cooperate and participate in the Western superpower's campaigns and activities. So in 2001 Libya abandoned its sponsorship of terrorism and instead got involved in counterterrorism and intelligence cooperation with the U.S. and the UN (Blanchard & Zanotti, 2011). In 2003, it admitted to and discontinued its WMD programs (Donnelly & Serchuk, 2004), and agreed to a Comprehensive Claims Settlement Agreement in line with the series of bombings in the 1980s that were heavily associated with Gaddafi's regime (Blanchard & Zanotti, 2011).

The United States was deeply wounded by the September 11 attacks by Bin Laden's terrorist group Al Qaeda in 2001. In line with the United States' grief and quest for justice, Muammar Gaddafi began to express "a willingness to join the global war on terror, identifying Bin Laden and Al Qaeda as a threat to his regime" (Donnelly & Serchuk, 2004, 2) and offered to provide the U.S. with intelligence regarding the jihadist group. In line with this emerging new partnership between the Gaddafi regime and the Bush administration against terrorism, negotiations regarding the United States' embargo against Libya started to surface.

Libya's counterterrorism efforts with the United States remained strong until the fall of Gaddafi's regime in late 2011. The country took "direct action to limit the activities of known Al Qaeda associates within its borders, including elements of its own Islamist opposition group allied with Al Qaeda" (Blanchard & Zanotti, 2011, 15). Libya also attended and participated in several conventions and procedures on dealing with terrorism, notably the International

103

Convention on the Suppression of the Financing of Terrorism. Libya's cooperation with the United States' fight against terrorism continued in the second half of the 2000s, prominently in 2008 when both countries dealt with several initiatives against the LIFG and members of Al Qaeda in the Maghreb region; and in 2010 and 2011 when Libya urged for a Trans-Sahara Counter Terrorism Partnership (TSCTP) with its neighbors which excluded Egypt and Sudan which remained uncooperative with the U.S. (Blanchard & Zanotti, 2011). In addition to these efforts, Gaddafi also contributed toward the release of Americans in the Philippines who were made hostages by a local Islamic group called the Abu Sayaff, as well as the release of Christian missionaries in Kabul who were taken by a Taliban group (Greavette, 2005).

Gaddafi further tried to rebuild Libya's international rapport and get on the United States' and its allies' good side. The Libyan leader admitted to the existence of the country's very own WMD program. He kept this a secret for decades, denying its existence despite U.S. and UK speculations since the 1970s. Before the U.S. and UK intelligence team slowly revealed Libya's purchase of WMD equipment from several suppliers around the globe, which included Pakistan and Malaysia, Gaddafi remained insistent that nuclear weapons were of no use to Libya, claiming that his government didn't have sufficient funds to pursue such a daring feat of owning its own WMD (Donnelly & Serchuk, 2004). This eventually changed upon the seizure of the German-owned cargo ship BBC China headed for Libya, which contained uranium-enriched centrifuges essential for WMD technologies and equipment. After being caught, the Libyan leader privately admitted by March 2003 of the existence of Libya's WMD and publicly announced this by December of the same year (Greavette, 2005). The reason behind Gaddafi's admission was his fear that his regime would end up like Saddam Hussein in Iraq, who was eventually overthrown from power and was executed shortly after by his own people. This action against Iraq was under "the Bush administration's determination to aggressively pursue terrorist groups, their state sponsors, and proliferators of weapons of mass destruction" (Donnelly & Serchuk, 2004, 1). Ironically,

Gaddafi's program was also on the list that the United States wished to destroy with its campaign against global terrorism before the Libyan leader wisely changed his ways just in time.

In line with Libya's public admission to its WMD programs and his promise to dismantle such programs, Gaddafi urged other countries, especially in the African continent and the Middle East, to follow his footsteps, as "Libya's newfound maturity is, in fact, evidence of the extent to which assertive American power, operating in conjunction with British allies, is transforming the political landscape in the Middle East" (Donnelly & Serchuk, 2004, 1). In the following years, the Libyan leader gradually removed all traces of his country's WMD and missile development programs to further strengthen U.S.-Libyan relations (Blanchard & Zanotti, 2011). In addition, the Libyan government signed a Comprehensive Test Ban Treaty (CTBT) in 2004 and agreed to the existence of a monitoring station within the country in order to ensure that Libya was following the conditions of the treaty (Greavette, 2005). Also in 2004, the U.S., UK and Libya formed a Trilateral Steering and Cooperation Committee (TSCC) that would further ensure the elimination of WMD and missile programs in the Mediterranean country (Blanchard & Zanotti, 2011).

By 2005, all of the remnants of Libya's nuclear weapons program were eliminated. This was followed in 2007 with the country selling its remaining uranium-based materials to other countries. But in 2008, Libya had trouble getting rid of its chemical weapons program and ended in the extension of the country's removal of all traces of its WMD by mid-2011. With the growing tensions within Libya in the beginning of 2011 and with the death of the Libyan leader in late 2011, the status of Gaddafi's promise with regards to his country's WMD is currently unknown.

The Gaddafi regime's continuous efforts to win the favor of the United States proved to be very difficult as the U.S. took its time in removing its embargos against Libya and removing the country from its list of enemies and terrorist nations. In 2003, the Libyan leader was involved in several peace talks and negotiations between rival African nations, as well as supporting and financing the United

Nations World Food Program aid flights to Sudan (Blanchard & Zanotti, 2011). In the second half of the 2000s, after the United States lifted most of its embargos against in Libya, Gaddafi's government involved itself with oil production and exploration with other countries, especially with Western oil investors and companies, in hopes to increase the country's oil revenues. The Libyan leader's changed political orientation also attracted several European and Asian nations in engaging and investing in Libya (Blanchard & Zanotti, 2011). By 2007, the country was made a temporary member of the UN Security Council in line with Gaddafi's full cooperation and participation with the international organization's campaign against terrorism. This led to the Colonel holding the Council's presidency in 2008 and 2009 (Blanchard & Zanotti, 2011).

Following Gaddafi's counterterrorism cooperation and his admitting and withdrawing Libya's WMD programs, the Bush administration urged the re-establishment of bilateral relations between Libya and the United States. This included a number of Executive Orders, provisions, and amendments. In 2004, the U.S. established a Liaison Office in Tripoli, removed most of its economic sanctions and travel bans against Libya, as well as unfroze the country's assets in the U.S. under Executive Order 13357 (Blanchard & Zanotti, 2011). Libya also opened a Libya Liaison Office in Washington, D.C. This was followed in 2005 by removing the state's arms bans, allowing Libya to purchase new weaponry and regain access to its confiscated arms. In 2006, the United States publicly announced its intention of completely reinstating its diplomatic relations with Libya and removing the country from the United States' list of states that sponsored terrorism and uncooperative nations (Blanchard & Zanotti, 2011). This led to the rebuilding of a U.S. Embassy in Tripoli. Later that year, the United States removed all of its remaining trade bans against Libya and removed the country from its terrorism titles. And finally in that same year, achieving the Gaddafi government's goal since 2001, the removal of Libya from the Iran-Libya Sanctions Act (Donnelly & Serchuk, 2004) was finalized.

As part of Gaddafi's reform, the United States and United Nations strongly pressed Gaddafi and Libya to admit to the series of bombings in the late 1980s which involved the deaths of American servicemen and civilians. Despite the denial Gaddafi's regime expressed on its involvement in the actions of several Libyans who were even part of the country's military and intelligence sector, he offered compensation to the victims of the bombings starting in 1999 (Donnelly & Serchuk, 2004). In 2006, the Libyan government met with the representatives of the 1986 LaBelle nightclub bombing victims a few times until eventually agreeing on a settlement. The series of payments by Libya to each of the victims was heavily monitored by the United States government. In 2008, Libya was found by a U.S. court directly responsible for the 1989 UTA Flight 772 bombing and Gaddafi's government was ordered to pay a total of $6 billion in damages to the six American victims' families and estates (Blanchard & Zanotti, 2011). The country also made a series of payments to the families of the French and German victims of both the LaBelle and UTA Flight 772 bombings.

The proper monitoring of payouts, especially for the victims of the Pan Am Flight 103 bombing in Lockerbie in 1988, was further strengthened under the Comprehensive Settlement Agreement issued under the Bush administration in 2008 and was carried out by the Obama administration until all sufficient payments were met by the Libyan government. It provided for "the establishment of a humanitarian settlement fund to receive donations sufficient to address the outstanding legal claims of U.S. terrorism victims and Libyan claims related to U.S. military strikes" (Blanchard & Zanotti, 2011, 9). Most of those donors were oil companies that Libya convinced to give to this fund. They had a vested interest in resolution so they could leverage oil contracts. In addition, the settlement agreement involved the removal of any pending U.S. cases against Libya before June 2006 once both the Libyan and U.S. government were able to settle all the agreed payments for the settlement fund. By 2008, a total of $536 million was collected for the Pan Am Flight 103 settlement, $283 million for the LaBelle settlement, and $681 million for compensating for the damages of other terrorist-related claims against Gaddafi's Libya (Blanchard & Zanotti, 2011).

Following the conviction of Abdel Basset Al Megrahi as being solely responsible for the 1988 Pan Am Flight 103 bombing, which killed a total of 270 people, U.S.-Libyan relations improved even further. Megrahi then appealed to the Scottish Criminal Cases Review Commission (SCCRC) to lessen the length of his imprisonment from a lifetime sentence to a 27-year sentence (Blanchard & Zanotti, 2011). This appeal was rooted in the questionable investigation behind the incident. The Popular Front for the Liberation of Palestine-General Command was then made a possible suspect behind the Lockerbie bombing (Blanchard & Zanotti, 2011). These alternative allegations and belief that Megrahi didn't have a proper defense led to Scottish courts granting Megrahi's appeals in 2006 and in 2007.

The formation of the Comprehensive Claims Settlement Agreement was based on Libya accepting its responsibility for its officials who were directly behind the series of bombings in the 1980s. But despite taking responsibility for Libya's agents, Gaddafi was never tried and always said he was innocent.

Despite the seemingly smooth flow of U.S.-Libyan relations, the growing partnership was met with several reemerging conflicts and hindrances. With the Scottish courts' granting of the convicted Megrahi's second appeal in 2007 and the surfacing of questions regarding the credibility of the findings of the Lockerbie bombing investigation, the defense team asked for the release of classified information and documents that were used as the case's primary evidence against the Libyan intelligence agent (Blanchard & Zanotti, 2011). This request was met with contradictory views within the courts and the parties involved with the case and the bombing. In 2008, Megrahi's team made a different appeal, asking the Scottish courts to approve his release on bail in line with his diagnosis of prostate cancer (Blanchard & Zanotti, 2011). This was eventually denied.

In 2009 following the diagnosis of Megrahi with prostate cancer, the Libyan government forwarded an application to the

Scottish government to allow for Megrahi to serve the remainder of his term in Libya under a prisoner transfer agreement with the UK. This was denied. However, Libya followed that denial up with a request for a compassionate release of Megrahi on the grounds of his terminal illness. This type of release is allowed under Scottish law. This request by Libya was met with criticism and outbursts from the families of several Lockerbie bombing victims. Despite this, the Scottish government later granted the release of the convicted Libyan when he was diagnosed by a doctor to allegedly have only three months to live, and was carried out without any agreement or settlement (Blanchard & Zanotti, 2011). Upon his release and his return to Libya, Megrahi was given a warm welcome like that of a hero, which in turn angered the Obama administration and the United Kingdom. They viewed the Libyan people's reaction as highly offensive, especially for the victims and their families.

Aside from the contradictory view of the United States and Libya with regards to Megrahi and the Lockerbie bombing, the two nations also had conflicting viewpoints in terms of the permanent establishment of U.S. military bases on African soil. In mid-2000, the Libyan government supported the establishment of the U.S. Africa Command (AFRICOM), which assured that the U.S. would merely hold a temporary presence on the continent just for the sake of ensuring security, but was generally rejected by other members of the Maghreb Union in a 2007 summit (Blanchard & Zanotti, 2011). Despite this hindrance for AFRICOM's establishment, both the United States and Libya agreed in continuing talks regarding the countries' military partnership in 2010 which was cut short in 2011 with the growing conflicts within Libya between Gaddafi's weakening government and growing opposition groups.

Once the United States started lifting its sanctions and embargos against its former enemy, Libya, starting in 2004, the U.S. under the Bush administration pushed for foreign assistance for the country. This was met by criticism from the majority of the U.S. Congress that wanted to maintain foreign assistance restrictions against Libya (Blanchard & Zanotti, 2011). Despite this, President Bush was able to remove all restrictions in helping out its growing ally in 2008. In his last year as the country's president, Bush submitted several financial assistance requests for Libya, which then were carried over to the Obama administration in 2009 (Blanchard & Zanotti, 2011). President Obama also requested a series of funding amounting to millions of dollars under the fiscal years 2010 and 2011, which unfortunately didn't push through.

During the last years of Gaddafi's regime, Libyan relations were continuously improving and growing with the United States under the Obama administration. But this was eventually jeopardized by the controversial release of Megrahi and the supposed influence of the United Kingdom government and the British oil company BP in his release.

In 2007, the Libyan National Oil Company (LNOC) and BP signed an energy exploration agreement worth an estimated worth $900 million, which happened during the Libyan visit of Tony Blair, then prime minister of the UK (Blanchard & Zanotti, 2011). These consecutive series of events led to the allegation that the British authorities' prisoner transfer agreement with Libya was being made applicable to the release of Megrahi in exchange for the country's oil wealth through BP, without consulting the Scottish authorities. This was immediately denied by the UK.

Upon the "compassionate release" of Megrahi in 2009, the United States pointed the blame for such a preposterous decision by the Scottish courts on the UK-Libyan prisoner transfer agreement initiated by UK officials and BP. This led four members of the U.S. Senate to write a letter addressed to Hillary Clinton, then the secretary of state, to investigate the British oil company's influence over the decisions by the UK and Scottish governments regarding the release of the convicted Libyan military official (Blanchard & Zanotti, 2011). This remained unproven as the allegations against BP lacked sufficient evidence.

From 2009 up to early 2011, Muammar Gaddafi's sons were quite active in Libya's foreign affairs, especially with the United States. Saif Al Islam was known for his push for reforms in Libya in contrast to his father's former stand on the country's economic, political and social situations. He was made the General Coordinator of the Popular Social Command that equaled the executive power of authority of the older Gaddafi over Libya (Blanchard & Zanotti, 2011). Due to Saif Al Islam's reformist view, rumors spread that he wasn't supported by his father's loyalists and followers who were strongly bent on a more conservative level of the Gaddafi regime's decades of rule of Libya. Despite the high position Gaddafi had given to his son, the younger Gaddafi remained inactive in exerting his new position's power over the country and its people, up until the fall of his father's regime shortly after.

Mutassim, another son of the Libyan leader, was also involved in Libyan politics and foreign relations. In 2009, he visited Washington and met with Secretary of State Hillary Clinton in order to discuss security cooperation between the two countries (Blanchard & Zanotti, 2011).

Many have speculated that the reasons behind the United States' and its allies' gradual acceptance of Libya from 1999 until the Gaddafi regime's end in late 2011 were a matter of benefits in terms of Libya's petrodollars by the billions. According to Lieutenant-Colonel Gordon Greavette (2005), this growing friendship was in line "with the evolving world energy situation, the Americans…realize that they and their European allies require Libyan oil, as well [as] Gaddafi's knowledge and influence in their War on Terror." This in turn benefited the Libyan leader and his country in ensuring the continuation of his control over Libya for several more years. But in the end, this relationship died down when the Gaddafi regime was slowly being weakened by its opposition within Libya's borders and eventually lost the acceptance and respect of the international community following a series of violent attacks and killings against Libyan protesters allegedly under the command of the Libyan dictator and his men.

Leadership Lessons

One of the most important attributes of a good leader is teachability. If you are to lead, you must know how to follow.

111

Gaddafi liked to read up on nations when he visited them, hoping he could prove himself brilliant by declaring some little-known fact. Yet, unfortunately this same interest didn't extend over into him being teachable about how to lead his country well. Years of sanctions against Libya didn't seem to have much influence on him. It wasn't until Gaddafi saw what happened to Saddam Hussein that he began to realize what could potentially happen to him, if he didn't change directions. So, slowly he began to change the way he had been doing business. The world community used his outstanding obligations in the terrorist cases to be the carrot and stick to get him to begin to cooperate. Where there had previously been antagonism, he slowly began to collaborate with the U.S. and other Western nations in the war on terror. As Gaddafi became more willing to work with other nations, he began to see how he and Libya could be welcomed back into the world community.

Chapter 9: The Libyan uprising

The beginning of 2011 for Gaddafi and his government was marked with growing protests from Libyan opposition groups and unsatisfied Libyan civilians. Libyans were growing tired of the Libyan leader's dictatorial ways, the worsening economic condition, as well as his continuous bastardization of the Islamic faith and his growing close relations with the Arab world's number one enemy, the United States of America. "The real rebels were the independents who had no western, eastern, foreign or Arab agendas. They also had no religious tendencies and they are the ones who liberated Libya" (Nuri Mismari, Alhayat.com interview, July 14, 2012).

Earlier in 2011, the National Conference for the Libyan Opposition, which was led by the National Libyan Salvation Front (NLSF) and other known Libyan opposition groups, joined forces with Internet-based protesters in planning a day of change in Libya beginning on February 17 (Blanchard & Zanotti, 2011). This growing opposition against the Libyan leaders was inspired by other recent movements in Libya's African and Arab neighbors, notably in Egypt which resulted in the forced resignation of the country's leader of thirty years, Hosni Mubarak, on February 11 of the same year. On February 17, the planned "day of rage" (Blanchard & Zanotti, 2011, 1), protesters by the hundreds rushed the streets of Libya's cities. According to limited media sources in the country, the protesters were handled by the Libyan government's armed forces with violence, the military attempting to break the crowd by firing at them and making use of tear gas, batons and water cannons. This shootout allegedly led to the death of 25 to more than 50 Libyans and angered the crowd even more as they began setting several buildings and other possessions of the government on fire.

By February 18, the protesters tripled by number as several thousand of them were able to occupy Libya's second largest city, Benghazi, as well as the northeastern area of the Cyrenaica region (Blanchard & Zanotti, 2011). This anti-Gaddafi crowd was also able to occupy a radio station where it strongly broadcasted against the government. According to Twitter update feeds during the day of the occupation of Benghazi and parts of Cyrenaica, Internet access and mobile communication was blocked in most of Libya (Blanchard & Zanotti, 2011). This continued with the Libyan government making use of its brute force through its armed forces and its "revolutionary committees" in violently weakening the intensifying opposition. In the same month, some of Gaddafi's officials were reported to be jailed after rejecting the Libyan leader's orders.

Due to the growing tensions not only in Libya, but also in Bahrain and Yemen, the United States and its allies were becoming worried but remained static in intervening in these countries for the first few months of the sudden upsurges against the political leaders and governments of these nations. The U.S. and its business sector started to become concerned about the detrimental effects that the ongoing conflict between Gaddafi and his Libyan opponents posed to the international oil market.

The increasing number of killings by Gaddafi's men sparked international criticism, especially from the United Nations and the North Atlantic Treaty Organization (NATO). By March, Gaddafi's opposition grew even stronger, forcing the Libyan leader to go into hiding, utilizing both Libyan and U.S. funds to support himself and the remainder of his regime. As the situation in Libya got bloodier and more chaotic, more and more civilians took refuge in neighboring countries such as Tunisia. With the growing intervention of the international community, Gaddafi's son Saif Al Islam warned the Western superpowers that if they got involved, his father would never give up his position as Libya's most powerful individual and would not give in to exile and other negotiations with them (Golovnina, 2011). The United States in turn replied to this threat that if Gaddafi continued to be stubborn, his hold on Libya could soon cause a civil war as his protesters seemed to be rapidly increasing by the thousands despite the series of brutal attacks by his troops leading to several deaths.

With the continuous resistance to the international community's pleas to avoid more bloodshed, the United Nations and the European Union declared sanctions against the Libyan dictator, his family and his close allies in the last week of February (*The*

114

Guardian, 2011). In March, with the National Transitional Council and its supporters successfully occupying Benghazi and neighboring areas, Gaddafi and his family went into hiding. By March 17, the UN implemented a no-fly zone over Libya in order to ensure the safety of the country's citizens from Gaddafi's armed forces (*The Guardian*, 2011). The city of Misrata eventually turned into a battlefield between U.S. fighter jets and Libya's heavily equipped forces. The U.S.'s very first air strikes occurred by mid-March in Benghazi in order to stop the Libyan leader's forces from retaking the city from the opposition groups. The regime's protesters bravely fought against Gaddafi's troops in Ras Lanuf despite being outnumbered and under-armed. By the end of March, a series of explosions and bombings transpired in Tripoli, Misrata and other cities and locations in Libya.

In April, NATO got involved in air strikes against Libyan forces. This led to the international organization's attack on Gaddafi's home in Libya's capital Tripoli, which allegedly killed the Libyan leader's youngest son, Saif al-Arab, and three of his grandchildren (*The Guardian*, 2011). In June, the series of reported killings of unarmed Libyan protesters and civilians by the Colonel's troops pushed the UN to forward the matter to the International Criminal Court (ICC). By June 27, arrest warrants were released by the ICC for Gaddafi, his son Saif Al Islam and his brother-in-law Abdallah al-Senussi who was the state's head of security, for their crimes against humanity (*The Guardian*, 2011). In addition, NATO was able to make more than 7,000 missile attacks in Libya in the single month of June. The months of June and July were highlighted by a series of meetings of different nations that discussed Libya's worsening situation. These meetings led to the rejection of the Gaddafi regime and the recognition of the leading National Transitional Council as Libya's rightful government body.

By August 22, Libyan rebels successfully entered Tripoli, which led to the Libyan leader calling out to his supporters via television and the radio to fight the opposition before they successfully took over Libya's capital (*The Guardian*, 2011). But the next day, August 23, during the Battle of Tripoli, Gaddafi's protesters were able to overpower Libyan troops and occupy and ransack the Libyan leader's residence located in the Bab al-Azziziya Barack. By August 29, Gaddafi's wife Safia, his only biological daughter Aisha and two of his sons fled to neighboring Algeria (*Hindustan Times*, 2011). One of his sons, Khamis, was killed while fighting against Libyan rebels around Tripoli on the same day.

In the start of September, conferences were held and attended by different political leaders in order to discuss their plans for rebuilding Libya once Gaddafi was eventually removed from power (*The Guardian*, 2011). Gaddafi's forces gradually weakened and peace was somehow taking a hold in the country as most of the Libyan leader's loyal followers were in hiding. The country was taken over temporarily by several opposition leaders during this time, with the supports of the U.S., UN, NATO and the rest of the international community. The oil ban against Libya was eventually lifted since there seemed to be no threat to the country's trade. Also in September, U.S. President Barack Obama urged the remaining loyal forces of Gaddafi to surrender, which the Libyan leader replied to through taunting NATO via a radio broadcast (*The Guardian*, 2011).

By October, the NTC and its Libyan supporters were able to arrest Mutassim, one of Gaddafi's sons, when he tried to escape. This was then followed by the successful capture of several prominent officials and loyalists to the Gaddafi regime. The Libyan leader was hiding in Sirte, one of his regime's last remaining refuges. But the NTC started to dominate the city and forced Gaddafi to escape to the Jarref Valley, his birthplace (*BBC News*, 2011).

The end of four decades of tyranny: Gaddafi's capture and death

On October 20, NATO troops were able to track down and spot Gaddafi's convoy of about 75 vehicles that were fleeing out of Sirte. He was with his son Mutassim and the Libyan army's head Abu Bakr Younis Jabr (*BBC News*, 2011). The NATO troops were able to destroy most of the vehicles but Gaddafi and some of his men

116

were able to escape the wreckage and run on foot. They hid in a nearby drainage pipes but were eventually surrounded and an exchange of gunshots filled the air, wounding the Libyan leader (*BBC News*, 2011). The whole capture and killing of Gaddafi was captured in a video footage by one of the NATO fighters and was immediately put on the web for everyone to see. The wounded Colonel could be seen with blood on different parts of his body and appeared to have been brutally beaten and inhumanely sodomized by his captors with a knife or a pole (*BBC News*, 2011). This led to mixed speculations and reactions from the international community on how Gaddafi actually died. Some regarded his capture and death as too overboard despite the Libyan leader's crimes, while others argued that he deserved his violent death (*The Guardian*, 2011).

The day of Gaddafi's death was International Conflict Resolution Day and I was scheduled to be a keynote speaker at a conference commemorating that day. So, within hours of the news of his death, I, being one of the few people to meet him, was once again telling my story on the news. It was surreal to say the least to think that on a day committed to talking about resolving conflict more peacefully, the man who had murdered my brother and countless others was found to have been pummeled to death by his own people. It left me conflicted, not wanting it to end that way, but realizing he gave few options. He refused to turn himself in or step down. Although it brought another level of closure for me knowing he could no longer hurt anyone, I saw the day being primarily about the Libyan people and their justice.

With regards to how Gaddafi actually died, a forensic report several days after his death revealed that the Colonel most probably died of bullet wounds he might have taken during the crossfire between his loyalist forces and the NATO fighters (*The Guardian*, 2011). This was supported by the NATO operation's commander but was challenged by a witness account that claimed Gaddafi was shot by one his captors in the abandon upon his capture and torture. The true story behind the Libyan leader's capture and death remained unknown as several versions of witness accounts and video footages surfaced which were quite contradictory to each other. The severed, decomposing bodies of Gaddafi and his son were dumped in a meat locker in Misrata that was open to public viewing (Malone, 2011). Five days after their death, the father and son tandem were buried in a secret place in the Saharan desert in order to avoid the Libyan dictator's followers from making his grave a shrine of worship of some sorts (*The Guardian*, 2011).

After this dramatic and bloody end to a 42-year regime, the United States made it a point to investigate Muammar Gaddafi's seemingly brutal killing at the hands of NATO fighters (Malone, 2011). Despite the contradictory claims of the former Libyan leader's captors, most Libyans didn't care about how Gaddafi died or how his corpse was treated because they were just happy that the months of civil war and bloodshed had finally come to an end.

On October 24, four days after his death, the former Libyan leader's will was circulated in the media. It stated that he wanted to be buried with the clothes he was wearing at the time of his death with his body untouched, as well as being buried in his birthplace in Sirte beside his family and relatives (Gaddafi, 2011), which didn't quite go as he wanted. Gaddafi also wanted his wife and children to be treated humanely.

Gaddafi's son Saif Al Islam remained on the run until his capture along the town of Obari in November 2011. He had hired a tour guide who I have worked with named Yousef to take him to the border. Although he was disguised, Yousef knew who he was and turned him in to rebel forces. He is currently facing a series of trials due to his crimes against humanity he shared with his father and some of his brothers.

The great Muammar Gaddafi who was able to remain as Libya's sole leader for 42 years joins the long line of what Dominic Sandbrook (2011) called the "twentieth-century tyrants" who were eventually overpowered by Western superpowers and international giants. Gaddafi's empire suffered the same tragic fate of other dictatorial and controversial leaders, especially in the Arab world and in Africa, who the former Libyan leader used to support in their reign of terror.

Most of the world may regard the death of Colonel Gaddafi as a huge relief, as yet another "international terrorist" has been officially erased from the face of the Earth, including the death of Iraq's Saddam Hussein and Al Qaeda's Osama Bin Laden. He was strongly regarded as "a cruel, arrogant, and cold-hearted killer" (Sandbrook, 2011) by his enemies and most of Libyan society. Despite the Gaddafi regime's mistakes, which led from one tragic event to another, the former Libyan dictator had some good points, especially during the first years of his reign over Libya.

In his will, Gaddafi wished that after his death, "the Libyan people should protect its identity, achievements, history, and the honorable image of its ancestors and heroes" (Gaddafi, 2011). The Libyan leader undeniably had a way with words but took measures in acting out his beliefs in mostly unconventional and outrageous ways. Gaddafi was also revolutionary and intelligent with his formulation of his own ideologies and philosophies which he wrote down in his infamous *Green Book* in the 1970s. He yearned for a sense of unity among nations he viewed as allies through pan-Arabism, pan-Africanism, socialism and populism, but instead was regarded as idealistic and was often ignored. The Colonel was also regarded as "honest, open, and straightforward in his support for terrorists, or as he viewed them, [as] guerillas and freedom fighters" (Greavette, 2005). And Gaddafi's by far most admirable trait was his charisma. At a very early age, he developed his very own viewpoint on politics, which he successfully utilized in influencing his classmates, who eventually became the Libyan dictator's long-time allies. This undeniable charm of his was characterized by some as "mystical," which led to Gaddafi gaining the trust and respect of Libya in the early years of his regime. In addition, his courage to stand up and go against the United States and its allies was quite remarkable, putting Libya on the map and getting the attention of the world as it used to be "a totally forgotten, beaten-down nation, and he changed that" (Greavette, 2005).

Gaddafi's mistakes were not necessarily on the ideals he had, which were generally quite reasonable and mind-changing. It was the manner in which he put these ideals of his to practice. Greavette (2005) further added that, "what [Gaddafi] lacked in practice, he more than made up for in theory." He often seemed to find himself in between capitalism and communism, which caused him great confusion and frustration throughout his rule over Libya. The Libyan leader also had to deal with the dilemma of following or going against certain norms, especially in the conservative Muslim nation he belonged to, in order to reach his goals for his country. These ideological struggles led to Gaddafi's ever-changing ideological beliefs which he instead relied on convenience and the given situation.

Leadership Lessons

Altruism is a little talked-about idea in leadership, but should be the main motivating force for someone to serve in public leadership. Altruism is the selfless concern for the well-being of others. Any altruistic purpose that Gaddafi may have had when he first led his revolution in 1969, was completely gone during the recent revolution. Instead, when the people rose up and asked for him to step down, he lashed out at them like a mad dog. There was little loyalty for Gaddafi even among his high-level officials and aides. One after the other, they switched sides and joined the revolution. In the end, he ended up hiring mercenaries from other nations to fight on his behalf.

The most important attribute of leadership that was lacking in Gaddafi and ultimately led to his demise was servant leadership. A lot has been written on the topic of servant leadership in recent years. But it isn't a new idea. It is rooted in the idea that leaders are given their position of leadership to steward for the good of the people they serve. This is especially true of public servants.

True leadership is servant leadership and is the exact opposite of how Gaddafi led. Real leaders see themselves as public servants who are called to represent the interests of the people. In a democracy governmental leaders are elected into office and chosen based on qualifications and how they will represent their constituents. If they don't do their job, the people have the ability to vote them out of office. This structure is inherently designed to prevent abuses of power that are present in a system of absolute rule like a dictatorship. Now it is true that monarchies and other forms of sovereign rule where there is no balance of power can also become abusive. So, in every leadership position, the true sign of a good leader is one who sees their role as a servant of the people. This is true in a kingdom where the king owns all the resources, or in a capitalistic nation. The leadership must be good stewards of the financial and human resources that are at their disposal.

The Libyan revolution was rooted in a desire to throw off the constraints of an oppressive dictator and search for freedom and democracy. For a true democracy to work, the power must be balanced among different governmental institutions to prevent corruption and abuse. In addition, the only way to prevent leaders from abusing power, is to allow the people to elect them into office.

Chapter 10: Libya after Gaddafi

Craig Black (2000) predicted more than a decade ago that Libya without Muammar Gaddafi upon the fall of his regime would result in worse conditions in Libya. This was because of the possibility of regional and religious factions within the country starting to emerge as each group would try to gain authority and control over Libyan territory, which the former Libyan leader greatly succeeded in repressing.

But Libya after the 42-year Gaddafi regime initially seemed to be facing a better, more productive future with the proclamation of the National Transitional Council (NTC) as its temporary government. In December 2011, a few months following the death of the former Libyan leader, the NTC established the country's executive body in preparation for the first free elections in Libya which happened in July 2012. Abdurrahim El-Keib was proclaimed as new Libya's new Prime Minister and Mustafa A.G. Abushagur as his Deputy Prime Minister. After the successful elections in line with the NTC's quest for constitutional democracy in Libya by 2013, a national assembly was effectively formed that will lead the country to a political transition for the better (*The Tripoli Post*, 2012). And the new cabinet of ministers were appointed. These ministers will then supervise the different sectors of the Libyan government such as Justice, Labor, Health, Interior, Energy, Communications and Information Technology, Education, Trade and Commerce, Foreign Affairs, Defense, Finance and many more.

Despite the new Libyan government's efforts to gradually get the country back on its feet, the General National Congress discovered in August 2012 that some of its members were involved in several criminal activities and were strong allies of Muammar Gaddafi. The Libyan representatives who were eventually banned from the national assembly were: Annifishi Abdussalam Abdul Manee, from Tarhouna; Salma Ekhail, who is a National Forces Alliance member from Zliten, and Ibrahim Mohamed Eddah from Obari, who is a member of the Libyan Party for Liberty and Development (*The Tripoli Post*, 2012). Five more Libyan representatives were under investigation. Once the 200-member national assembly was finalized, the very young Libyan government could start with drafting the country's very first constitution under democracy.

With the complete removal of international sanctions and embargos against Libya after the fall of the Gaddafi and the rise of a new Libya under the temporary supervision of the NTC, the country's economy has rapidly improved in a year's time. According to the *Business Monitor International*, Libya was the fastest growing economy for the year 2012 (Dabrowska, 2012). This was projected when the country's GDP grew a staggering 58.9 percent following the improvement of its oil industry, especially in its domestic oil production and exploration, which has recently attracted more and more foreign investors. Aside from oil, the *Business Monitor International* also saw the potential of Libya's hydrocarbon production in further ensuring the economy's continuous growth in the next ten years (Dabrowska, 2012). In line with this, Libya's biggest oil refinery located in Ras Lanuf was reopened in September 2012, after being closed for a year. The refinery allegedly was able to produce more than 200,000 oil barrels in a single day. Following the reopening of the Ras Lanuf oil refinery, Libya's oil revenue was expected by the Libyan National Oil Corporation (NOC) to reach a value of about $55 billion by the end of 2012 (*The Tripoli Post*, 2012). This was in line with Libya's daily average barrel count reaching more than one million at an average price of a hundred dollars per barrel. In late 2013, Libya was producing 700,000 barrels a day (Bloomberg, September 29, 2013).

But this billion-dollar oil industry is a great responsibility, requiring transparency from the government to ensure that Libya's oil revenues will be properly distributed and allocated to the state's projects for the benefit of the country's citizens. Corruption and greed has been a common issue in the previous governments that handled Libya's massive oil wealth. That is why despite Libya being proclaimed as the "fastest growing economy in the world," it will always be right and true governance and leadership in the end that will dictate the real outcome and situation of Libya once it gets back

123

on its feet in terms of the current reformation of the country's politics, after being under Gaddafi for 42 years.

Sadly, as was predicted, Libya has become a seedbed for terrorists and extremists. Terrorist attacks have become daily occurrences, such as the event resulting in the death of U.S. Ambassador Chris Stevens and his staff.

I have been back to Libya several times since the revolution. After the assassination most of the NGOs had pulled out of Libya. New leaders came into power and other leaders who were close associates of Gaddafi were voted ineligible to serve. The continued attacks have spiraled into a general state of lawlessness with militias filling the security vacuum as best they can. Where one bad guy worked as leader, several more bad guys are seeking to take his place, at whatever cost.

Conclusion

As I have traveled on this journey, one of the most important priorities I had for myself was finishing well because I believe that is one of the most important leadership principles. Yet the finish line was elusive. How long, I would ask, must I continue this mission? Will I ever be able to put this season to rest?

On the day Gaddafi was killed, I found out the news as I prepared to present the keynote speech on International Conflict Resolution Day. There I stood, talking about my journey of forgiveness and reconciliation once more but with a new twist, news that Gaddafi was dead. The news crews crowded the room to hear my personal account once more.

Is this finally the closure I deep down so desperately long for? I was tired both spiritually and emotionally, and even physically. The stress of a journey like this, can take its toll on a woman in many ways. It is like being in a battle that never ends. I have sacrificed a lot to walk down this lonely path.

The real release to finish this chapter did not come until 2013. As I began the year, it became clear that this would be the last leg on this part of my journey. As the 25th anniversary happens on December 21, 2013, I will officially bring this chapter to a close for my life. Much has happened in the last 25 years that I can be proud of. There was a conviction, acceptance of responsibility by the Libyan government and payment of civil damages. The convicted bomber Abdel Basset Al Megrahi is dead and so is Muammar Gaddafi. Libya is free from the clutches of the brutal dictator. My influence has extended around the world, and will likely continue. But as for the Lockerbie chapter and story, it is time to move on.

In the spring of 2013 a reporter from the BBC named Glenn Campbell called me. He had in prior years interviewed me on more than one occasion and done a great job of capturing the heart of my work.

"The BBC has asked me to do a documentary on the 25th anniversary of Lockerbie and I want to take a much different approach and feature your work and journey," he said.

"What does the 25th anniversary mean to you?" he probed.

No one had ever asked me that question before. So being a person who tends to process as I speak, I had not really fully processed it.

"To me, the 25th anniversary is about closure of this chapter. Twenty-five years is a very long time to carry something like this. I need for this chapter to be over," I said.

As the words came out of my mouth it became very clear to me what I needed.

"I have no regrets. I started this journey when I was 18 years of age, never having a clue where it would take me. It was just out of a desire to make my brother's death not be in vain. But it wasn't necessarily the path I would have chosen for myself. But for years Lockerbie has defined me. Imagine every time people introduce you to another person they say, 'This is Lisa, her brother died in the 1988 Lockerbie terrorist attack and she met with Gaddafi.'"

Glenn listened intently as I processed through my thoughts and feelings. I didn't know it until that moment, but I desperately needed that. It was cathartic.

In early October of 2013, the BBC flew me to Washington, D.C., for a series of interviews for the documentary. They had asked me to ask Ambassador Aujali to be a part of an interview as well. He had recently resigned from his position as Ambassador, but graciously agreed. He invited me and the film crew to his home in McLean, Virginia, to conduct the interview.

It was a chilly fall day in the D.C. area as the colors had already changed and there was a dampness in the air. I stood outside with the cameraman and producer as we shot multiple takes of my walking up to Ambassador Aujali's front door and him coming out to meet me. It was very surreal as I had not seen him in over a year and a half, since the revolution ended and Gaddafi was killed. When he opened the door to greet me he had a big smile on his face. It looked authentic and it calmed the nerves I was feeling.

The whole process was completely unnatural. There we were trying to share a personal moment and talk about our history, but in a very staged way. I now understand very much what reality show artists and actors feel like. They must have shot six takes of my finger pressing the doorbell of Ambassador Aujali's house. It was funny.

Where I entered into the Ambassador's house I felt more settled. The rest of his family was in another room, so the film crew could do their work. We both settled onto the couch for our talk. As I sat there, I was reminded of how kind Ambassador Aujali had been in our first meeting years earlier, shortly after the Libyan government opened their office in Washington, D.C. A lot had happened since then.

For many years we would have meetings; he came to Colorado for our charity golf scramble and we played golf together, and I would attend receptions every year for the anniversary of Gaddafi's revolution. But in those meetings and in our talks we often had to talk around certain issues related to Lockerbie and Gaddafi. I wondered what the Ambassador might share now that his life was no longer in jeopardy by Gaddafi.

As we sat on the couch chatting, our initial conversation was more superficial. Ambassador Aujali asked about my mother who he had met years before at a charity golf event we had to benefit kids in Libya with HIV/AIDS.

"I really appreciated back in 2004 when I reached out to you and wanted to find a way to connect with Libya and how you helped me go there and, and to get into the country and then just from there to be able to take this bad experience and allow me to turn it into something good by helping in Libya," I said.

He nodded.

"This twenty-five year period has been more about taking something sad and turning it into something good. Just to be able to help the Libyan people has been incredibly meaningful because they have gone through their own trials and tribulations. So I want to thank you for that," I said.

"I really was surprised to be approached by a family member of a victim of the Pan Am, you know, at that time. And it was, it was really a very forward step to the right direction that, all the pain, all the suffering you have, and even with that you are willing to have a good relation with the Libyan people," he said.

"And I was really surprised and really admired your courage, when you came to the Embassy and we talk and then we started to connect with each other and participate in the golf tournament you organized that time to help the Libyan people, you know, to help the Libyan children actually and you collect that amount of money, $25,000."

"Yes," I said as I smiled.

"We do appreciate this very much. And I think it was really a surprise to the Libyan government too that a family member of the Pan Am 103 wanted to come to Libya and see the Libyans and that's, that's a great step by you, I think," he said.

"I remember my first trip there in 2005, it was when I really started to hear about the stories of the people in Libya and I knew that I could maybe have an impact in some small way. Since the revolution, doing conflict resolution training and leadership development and training in ethics and inner-cultural intelligence. These kinds of programs help to break down the barriers that we have," I said.

"And you are one of the very important people who build this bridge, you know, since 2004 when we start talk to each other and we start this relation for, not for business, not for interest, just for interests of the two nations, two people who want to know more about each other and it's a great job, you know," he said.

After our exchange, Glenn Campbell asked Ambassador Aujali very pointed questions about his thoughts about Lockerbie and whether Gaddafi was the mastermind.

"I cannot exclude Gaddafi is involved in this kind of dirty business unfortunately. He had no value for the human rights, for human lives. Nobody could really change his mind, even close friends or close assistants. When he decided to do something I think he will do it. It is unfortunate incident happening, that time Gaddafi is, he believe that he is the right challenger to the West, he believe that he can hit back, he believe that they, the, the West they should recognize his power, his influence, his intelligence, all these kind of things. And I think the main issue for Gaddafi, he wanted attention bad or good, it didn't matter to him.

"It was not clear to me because I am not sure Libya could do this by themselves. On other hand, Gaddafi he had a criminal mind and even if you don't expect it, it can happen. He shot down his own Libyan airline jet with more than one hundred seventy Libyans just to prove to the West how much the sanctions hurt the Libyan economy and the Libyan people's life," he said.

"Although Libya did accept responsibility for its agents, for Abdel Basset Al Megrahi when he was convicted of the bombing. Was that an admission of guilt or was it something more for political convenience?" Glenn Campbell said.

"Well, I think this is for political convenience after the invasion of Iraq. And I think Gaddafi saw the things very clear. And I believe that there is no time for him, no place to make any other maneuvers, to make any other confrontation with the West."

"So if Gaddafi accepted responsibility for Megrahi, for political reasons, what about the truth?" Glenn Campbell asked.

"God knows the truth. I think there are some other names that were mentioned beside Libya, you know, that Libya and some other countries are involved in this incident," Ambassador Aujali said.

"This has been written in the media and been mentioned many times, but maybe Libya was the weakest, the weakest link, and because of Gaddafi's arrogance and because of his policy, attitude toward the international community and the world, you see he paid the price for that.

"Abdul Senussi, the one who is under arrest now, one hundred percent knows the truth. You have to interview him to get the facts from his mouth."

There I had it, the closest thing to the truth as I would likely hear in my lifetime. It felt really good to hear Ambassador Aujali tell what he knew and be very honest for the first time, where he could not before. I left that meeting in a more peaceful place than I had in years before. It was also helpful to hear what it was like to serve as a leader under Gaddafi's regime. In the midst of all the deception that had been perpetrated over the course of many years, it had become clear to me that there were many good people who served as leaders under Gaddafi and tried their best to make a difference in the midst of his corruption.

"We felt, even as a diplomat that we were not welcome in any country. People kept their distance from us. It really hurt. But other reasonable people understood you have to do your job, to help the Libyan people. It was very tough," Ambassador Aujali said.

Closure

The death of my brother when I was 18 impacted my life far more than any other experience or event. Tragedies can have that effect on people. Some never find the courage to move beyond their loss and end up spiraling into destructive behavior to cope. But for others, the only way to transform the loss is to turn it into something positive. We all have choices in life and those choices impact our future. In a split second we are forced to make decisions about how we will respond in the midst of trials and tribulations, without a clear idea of the impact those decisions will have.

When Gaddafi started his journey, he too had a choice. He started out with an idealistic vision for the future of Libya and then went the path of the dark side. In response to his evil against my family, I chose to follow the light.

Gaddafi had always wanted to be the leader of a great nation. Instead, he died without ever making any significant impact on the world in a death that was befitting a man of his character. He was beaten to death at the hands of the people he was called to serve. There was no royal funeral procession or state events. Instead, he was spit upon, disfigured and then buried in an unmarked grave in the desert with no last rites or funeral.

He will be remembered as a rapist, murderer, tyrant, dictator, oppressor, and a devil.

As I close this chapter of my journey, what I am left with is a tremendous legacy of doing good in the midst of evil. I have looked at Gaddafi's life as an example of how not to lead. His life has taught me a lot about the importance of the right heart motives in leadership and how easy it is to get off track if you do not have the right foundation. This journey has shown me that one person can take on the forces of evil and come out triumphant. One person can make a difference in this world if we are willing to pay the price. So, as I end this part of my journey, I am tremendously thankful for the opportunity that my brother's death has given me. It is an opportunity I never would have had to impact the world in ways that I have. I am thankful for all that I have learned through this experience and what I will take into my future endeavors. The simple accolades I have that I finished well is I sense that my brother Ken and God are looking down from heaven, smiling and saying, "Well done!

References:

A look at the fate of Gaddafi's family. (2011, November 20). *Hindustan Times*. Retrieved from http://www.hindustantimes.com/world-news/Africa/A-look-at-the-fate-of-Gaddafi-s-family/Article1-771590.aspx.

Black, C. R. (2000). *Deterring Libya: The strategic culture of Muammar Qaddafi*. Maxwell Air Force Base, AL: USAF Counter-proliferation Center.

Blanchard, C. M., & Zanotti, J. (2011). *Libya: Background and U.S. relations*. Congressional Research Service, 1-41.

Chmatelli, Maher (2013, September 23). Libya Daily Oil Production Exceeds 700,000 barrels, Awami says. Bloomberg News. Retrieved from http://www.bloomberg.com/news/2013-09-29/libya-daily-oil-production-exceeds-700-000-barrels-awami-says.html

Dabrowska, K. (2012, September 1). Libyan Economy the Fastest Growing in the World. *The Tripoli Post*. Retrieved from http://www.tripolipost.com/articledetail.asp?c=2&i=9122.

Donnelly, T., & Serchuk, V. (2004). Beware the "Libyan Model." *American Enterprise Institute for Public Policy Research*, 1-8.

Elgood, G., & Stamp, D. (2011, October 21). Gaddafi's children in exile, on the run, or dead. *Reuters*. Retrieved from http://www.reuters.com/article/2011/10/21/us-libya-gaddafi-family-idUSTRE79K3B520111021.

Gaddafi, M. (2011). *This is my will: Muammar Gaddafi*. Retrieved from http://hamsayeh.net/world/1285-this-is-my-will muammar-gaddafi.html.

Golovnina, M. (2011, March 1). U.S. warns of civil war in Libya

unless Gaddafi goes. *Reuters*. Retrieved from
http://www.reuters.com/article/2011/03/01/us-libya-protests-idUSTRE71G0A620110301.

Greavette, G. (2005). "Great aspirations: The fall and rise of Muammar Qaddafi." Unpublished doctoral dissertation, Tri-University History Program, Wilfrid Laurier University, Ontario.

Kushner, H. W. (2003). *Encyclopedia of Terrorism*. Thousand Oaks, CA: Sage Publications, Inc.

Libya New Cabinet Expected by September 8, Three Congress Members Banned. (2012, August 30). *The Tripoli Post*. Retrieved from http://www.tripolipost.com/articledetail.asp?c=1&i=9109.

Malone, B. (2011, October 20). Gaddafi killed in hometown, Libya eyes future. *Reuters*. Retrieved from http://www.reuters.com/article/2011/10/20/us-libya-idUSTRE79F1FK20111020.

Mismari, Nuri. Interview with Alhayat.com, July 14, 2012.

Muammar Gaddafi: How he died. (2011, October 31). *BBC News*. Retrieved from http://www.bbc.co.uk/news/world-africa-15390980.

Qaddafi, M. A. (1988). *The Green Book*. Amherst, NY: Prometheus Books.

Sandbrook, D. (2011, October 22). The end of the twentieth-century tyrants, and the dawn of the multinational giants. *Daily Mail*. Retrieved from http://www.dailymail.co.uk/debate/article-2052035/Gaddafi-dead-End-20th-century-tyrants-dawn-multinational-giants.html.

Simons, G. (1996). *Libya: The Struggle for Survival*. New York, NY: St. Martin's Press.

Sullivan, K. L. (2009). *Muammar Al-Qaddafi's Libya*. Minneapolis, MN: Twenty-First Century Books.

Timeline: Libya's civil war. (2011, November 19). *The Guardian*. Retrieved from http://www.guardian.co.uk/world/2011/nov/19/timeline-libya-civil-war.

Victim's families call for investigation into 'crash' of Libyan plane. (2013, April 1). Tripoli Post. Retrieved from http://www.tripolipost.com/articledetail.asp?c=1&i=9712

About The Author

Lisa Gibson, JD is a #1 International Best Selling Author, an attorney, internationally acclaimed conflict and forgiveness expert, mediator, and certified and motivational speaker. She is an award winning and best selling author of *Life In Death: A Journey From Terrorism To Triumph; The Expert Success Solution; Releasing The Chains: Timeless Wisdom On How To Forgive Anyone For Anything and the audio series Learning To Forgive: Your Pathway To Inner Peace.*

Lisa lost her brother in the 1988 terrorist bombing of Pan Am flight 103 over Lockerbie, Scotland. Rather than succumbing to bitterness she met with and forgave former Libyan leader Muammar Gaddafi, the mastermind behind that terrorist attack. Because of Lisa's personal experience, she now specializes in cross-cultural conflict resolution and has trained thousands of government, business, healthcare and nonprofit leaders in conflict-ridden countries in how to forgive and resolve conflicts more effectively. She has been featured in such media outlets as CNN, ABC, NBC, CBS, FOX, BBC, MSNC, Wall Street Journal, USA Today, New York Times, and countless others.

In 2013 Lisa was given the distinguished honor of being chosen as an "Exemplar Of Love And Forgiveness In Governance" by Fetzer Institute and the School For Conflict Analysis And Resolution" and in 2010 was chosen as one of Ten Outstanding Young Americans by the US Junior Chamber Of Commerce.

Visit www.conflictcoach.biz/freetraining/ to download your free audio training.